from the field

PHEASANTS
forever
The Habitat
Organization

Better Homes and Gardens®
Test Kitchen

Hunters commemorate more than **25 years** of Pheasants Forever with recipes, photos and stories, plus favorite recipes from the Better Homes and Gardens Test Kitchen

Dear Conservationist,

We hope you enjoy this compilation of great recipes and stories!

Nothing accompanies a successful day in the field quite like a hearty meal in the company of friends and family, with stories running long after the fork and glass have been set down. It's a tradition engrained in the fabric of America, and one we at Pheasants Forever hope to continue forever.

And while we could never include all the amazing and diverse recipes from all our dedicated Pheasants Forever members and upland bird enthusiasts, we think this 25th anniversary cookbook offers just enough to whet your appetite.

Most importantly, this book celebrates what has made Pheasants Forever such a successful organization in its first quarter century of existence – you. Our dedicated volunteer members are the lifeblood of Pheasants Forever, and we owe a great deal of thanks to you for taking us where we've been, and leading us to where we're going.

Like a memorable hunt, a fine meal of freshly prepared game is one that is never forgotten. Just like your first double and your best bird dog, we have a feeling that a few of these recipes and stories will be right up there amongst your favorites. Enjoy!

Think habitat,

Howard K. Vincent
Pheasants Forever
President and CEO

SUCCESSFUL FARMING

from the field

PHEASANTS
forever
The Habitat
Organization

Custom Publishing Manager: Diana Willits
Editor: Lisa Prater
Designer: Brian Shearer
Copy Editor: Paula Barbour
Editor In Chief: Loren Kruse

Successful Farming®/Meredith Corporation
Publisher: Scott Mortimer
Vice President/Group Publisher: Tom Davis
Senior Vice President: Doug Olson

Pheasants Forever
President and CEO: Howard K. Vincent
VP of Corporate Relations & Marketing: Joseph J. Duggan
VP of Governmental Affairs: David E. Nomsen
VP of Field Operations: Richard E. Young
Chief Financial Officer: James Koerber
VP of Education and Outreach: Cheryl K. Riley
VP of Development: David Bue

Pheasants Forever, 1783 Buerkle Circle, Saint Paul, MN 55110
www.pheasantsforever.org

From The Field (ISBN 978-0-696-24103-1) is published by
Meredith Corporation, 1716 Locust Street, Des Moines, IA 50309-3023.

Printed in USA

Table of Contents

25 years of Pheasants Forever
looking back, looking ahead

Hunting pheasants and other upland birds is a way of life for many men and women across the country. It's a passion we enjoy with our spouses, with friends, and with our entire families. Hunting trips are plotted years in advance, wedding dates are set so as not to interfere with hunting season, and puppies are lovingly trained with the hope they will one day flush the perfect bird.

But without plentiful habitat, none of this would be possible. Pheasants Forever has tirelessly worked to improve and increase upland bird habitat, and to return thousands of acres to their natural state, providing a haven for the birds and other wildlife.

It's because so many of us get chills when we think of the sights, sounds and smells associated with pheasant hunting, that we are so pleased to bring you this collection of recipes, photographs and stories from hunters around the country. We know you share our enthusiasm, we thank you for 25 years of support, and we look forward to a bright future!

From Humble Beginnings

Pheasants Forever was founded when Dennis Anderson, the outdoor editor for a Minnesota newspaper, wrote an emotional plea for hunters and habitat enthusiasts to preserve their state's upland bird habitat. The year was 1982.

Because the government had urged farmers to plant from fencerow to fencerow, valuable habitat was destroyed, and game birds found it more and more difficult to survive Minnesota's harsh winters. It was lack of habitat, Anderson and others believed, that was leading to the pheasant's decline in his state.

After receiving more than 100 letters and 50 phone calls from across Minnesota, Anderson published another article in which he first named the group of concerned citizens "Pheasants Forever." He called for a pheasant stamp to pay farmers to manage marginal acres for pheasant habitat, and said the group also would work with wildlife biologists.

"I've come to realize," Anderson wrote in his column, "that we, each of us, have the opportunity to make a difference, and for the better. I think the low-water mark on habitat loss has finally been reached. Pheasants and other upland birds now have friends whom, together, will ensure their well-being."

Twenty-five years later, Pheasants Forever (PF) has more than 100,000 members in more than 630 chapters in 29 states, plus chapters in sister organization Pheasants Forever-Canada. More than 20 wildlife biologists are employed around the U.S., with a growing cadre of habitat specialists. The group is renowned for working with landowners, and it has worked to continue the federal Conservation Reserve Program, which safeguards millions of acres of American grasslands.

Pheasants Forever held its first annual banquet in 1983, raising more than $20,000 to get the organization started. Jeff Finden, one of Dennis Anderson's co-workers, helped found the organization and organize the banquet, and he later became PF's first executive director. The group's headquarters was located in Finden's basement in White Bear Lake, Minnesota, until 1986, when PF moved just across town.

In 1987, Howard Vincent signed on as the organization's finance director, and became chief executive officer when Finden retired in 2000.

The policy of allowing chapters to keep all the funds they raise is key to Pheasants Forever's growth and local habitat success. The national office is funded by memberships, merchandise sales, corporate partners and fundraisers. But money raised locally stays with each chapter to improve habitat in their areas.

"We understand our core mission is habitat and education, but at the same time we're looking for better and more efficient ways to achieve those goals," Vincent says. "Keep your eyes on Pheasants Forever. There's much more to come."

For my dad, my husband, and my sons. And in memory of my father-in-law, below, who truly loved the land.   —Lisa Foust Prater

About This Book

When Pheasants Forever celebrated its 25th anniversary, the organization's leaders wanted to commemorate the occasion with a cookbook. They turned to the experts at the Better Homes and Gardens Test Kitchen, and the editorial staffs at *Successful Farming* and *Living the Country Life* magazines, to turn that dream into a reality.

We sought input from Pheasants Forever members and other wildlife and habitat enthusiasts from across the country, and were rewarded with hundreds of delicious recipes, plus wonderful photographs and stories from the field.

Throughout the book, you'll also find wild game favorites from Better Homes and Gardens Test Kitchen, which creates and tests recipes for many of the Meredith Corporation publications. When you see the Better Homes and Gardens logo (above) you'll know that recipe came from our kitchen — for you to enjoy in yours.

Bon appétit!

The Western Midwest

We begin our hunting and eating tour of the nation where Pheasants Forever got its start 25 years ago. In Minnesota — and in the other states that make up the western Midwest — hunting is serious business. And these folks are as inventive and crafty in the kitchen as they are in the field.

> # It is not what we have that will make us a great nation — it is the way in which we use it.

Theodore Roosevelt, July 4, 1886, Dakota Territory
(As president, Roosevelt set aside 230 million acres of federal land for conservation projects.)

Pheasant Stuffing Pie

Sharon Vanderwilt, Orange City, Iowa

Ingredients:

- 1 8-oz. pkg. stuffing mix
- ¾ cup chicken broth
- ½ cup butter, melted
- 1 egg, beaten
- 1 3-oz. can sliced mushrooms
- 2 Tbsp. flour
- ½ onion, chopped
- 1 Tbsp. butter
- 1 jar chicken gravy
- 1 tsp. Worcestershire sauce
- ½ tsp. thyme
- 3 cups pheasant, cooked and cubed
- 1 cup frozen peas
- 2 Tbsp. pimento, diced
- 1 Tbsp. parsley flakes
- 4 oz. Colby or American cheese

Step 1: Combine stuffing mix, chicken broth, melted butter and egg, press into 9-inch pie pan to make a crust.

Step 2: Combine mushrooms and 2 tablespoons flour; set aside.

Step 3: Sauté onion in butter. Add mushroom mixture to skillet along with remaining ingredients except cheese. Heat until warm, then spoon into crust. Bake 30 minutes at 375° F. Top with cheese and return to oven until cheese melts.

Pheasant with Morels Over Pasta

Rick Leier, Circle Pines, Minnesota

Ingredients:

- 2 pheasants, boned
  Morel mushrooms (as many as you have available)
- 2 cups brandy
- 1 pint heavy cream
  Butter
  Nutmeg

Step 1: In a heavy pan, brown the boned pheasants in butter until golden brown.

Step 2: Add brandy, heat until bubbling. Ignite the brandy and let the flames go out on their own. (Take care not to ignite range hood or other items near stovetop.) Cover and simmer 20 to 30 minutes until tender. Remove meat from the pan, cover and keep warm.

Step 3: In a separate pan, sauté Morels in butter until crispy, but do not burn them.

Step 4: Add Morels and butter to leftover liquid in the pheasant pan. Add cream. Simmer until it thickens enough to coat a spoon. Add nutmeg, salt and pepper to taste.

Step 5: Place the pheasant on a platter, cover in sauce. Add additional cream to extra sauce and serve on the side, if desired. Serve with pasta or brown rice.

Pheasant Bruschetta Bake

Barbara Fuller, Corning, Iowa

Ingredients:

- 1 14.5-oz. can diced tomatoes
- 1 6-oz. package seasoned stuffing mix, chicken flavored
- ½ cup water
- 2 cloves garlic, minced
- 1½ lbs. pheasant breast, skinless, cut into bite-size pieces
- 1 tsp. dried basil leaves
- 1 cup Mozzarella cheese, shredded

Step 1: Place tomatoes, stuffing mix and water in a bowl and stir to combine.

Step 2: Place pheasant chunks on bottom of 9×13-inch baking dish. Sprinkle with basil and cheese. Top with stuffing mixture. Bake 30 minutes at 400° F. Makes 6 servings, about 1 cup each.

Pheasant with Green Chilies

Sandi Witt, Hoisington, Kansas

Ingredients:

- 1 to 2 pheasants, deboned and cut into serving-size pieces
  Flour or seasoned flour
  Salt and pepper to taste
  Butter
- 1 4-oz. can chopped green chilies (or more to taste)
- 1 onion, diced
- 1 can cream of mushroom or cream of celery soup
  Cream, milk or water

Step 1: Dust bird pieces in flour, salt and pepper.

Step 2: Heat butter and brown pieces. Place browned pieces in casserole dish.

Step 3: Brown onion, chilies and anything else you'd like to add (for example, celery if using cream of celery soup; mushrooms if using cream of mushroom soup). Add soup to mixture and thin to desired consistency using cream, milk or water. Pour over pheasant pieces.

Step 4: Bake at 325° F. for two hours. Serve atop fettuccine Alfredo.

English Pheasant Oscar

John Linquist, Pheasants Forever Regional Representative, Sibley, Iowa

Ingredients:
- 1 pheasant breast
- 1 English muffin
- 4 asparagus spears
- ½ cup crab meat, fresh or imitation
- 1 pkg. Hollandaise sauce mix
- Butter

Step 1: In a sauce pan, prepare Hollandaise sauce according to package directions.

Step 2: Prepare pheasant breast for grilling by seasoning to taste. Place on grill and cook slowly until meat is done in the middle. Remove from heat.

Step 3: Apply a light coating of butter to English muffin, and brown buttered-side-down in a skillet. At the same time, steam asparagus on stovetop until tender.

Step 4: If using canned or imitation crab meat, drain and heat. If using fresh crab, cook.

Step 5: Place grilled English muffins on plate. Add grilled pheasant breast on top of muffins. Add asparagus, and sprinkle with crab meat. Pour the Hollandaise sauce generously on top. Serves 1.

Pheasant Parmesan

Walda Rogers, Pheasants Forever Chapter Treasurer, Lake McKenna, North Dakota

Ingredients:
- 1 pheasant breast
- Garlic powder
- Onion powder
- Pepper
- 1 pkg. Panko Japanese breading
- 1 pkg. spaghetti
- 1 jar canned spaghetti sauce or your favorite homemade sauce
- ½ cup grated Parmesan or 2 slices mozzarella cheese

Step 1: Slice pheasant breast into ½-inch-thick strips. Season to taste with garlic powder, onion powder and pepper.

Step 3: Following the package directions, coat meat with Panko Japanese breading. Set aside.

Step 4: Prepare spaghetti and sauce according to directions.

Step 5: Deep fry or pan fry pheasant until crispy, 2 to 3 minutes. Coating will get very crisp and meat will remain moist and tender.

Step 6: Place spaghetti and sauce on platter. Top with pheasant. Sprinkle grated Parmesan or place mozzarella slices on top. Place under broiler until cheese is melted.

Creamed Pheasant Legs

Sheila Sandness, Bismarck, North Dakota

Ingredients:
- 12 pheasant legs
- 1 bay leaf
- 2 tsp. allspice
- 1 onion, chopped
- Salt and pepper to taste
- ¼ cup flour
- 1 Tbsp. sugar
- ½ cup whipping cream
- Additional whipping cream

Step 1: Combine pheasant legs, bay leaf, allspice, onion, salt and pepper in a large pot and cover with water. Stew legs until meat is tender and falls from bone.

Step 2: Strain broth and set aside. Remove meat from legs and pull tendons from meat. Put meat and broth back into pot and bring to a boil.

Step 3: Combine flour, sugar and ½ cup whipping cream in a bowl. Add 1 cup of broth from pot.

Step 4: Add flour and cream mixture to the pot. Add additional cream to taste. More flour and sugar may be added if broth is too watery.

Step 5: Heat through and serve over homemade bread or mashed potatoes.

Pheasant Dinner in a Bag

Mary Brau, St. Paul, Minnesota

Ingredients:
- 1 oven cooking bag, regular or large size
- 1 Tbsp. flour
- 1 pkg. (¾ – 1 oz.) dry chicken gravy mix
- 1 cup water
- 4-8 pheasant pieces
- Salt
- Pepper
- Paprika
- 2-3 potatoes, peeled and cut into chunks
- 2 medium carrots, sliced
- 1 stalk of celery, sliced
- ½ onion, cut into chunks

Step 1: Shake flour in oven bag. Add gravy mix and water; squeeze bag to mix ingredients. Place bag in 9×13-inch baking pan.

Step 2: Place pheasant pieces on a platter. Sprinkle with salt, pepper and paprika to taste.

Step 3: Add meat and vegetables to bag and close with nylon tie. Cut 5 half-inch slits in the top of the bag. Bake at 350° F. until pheasant is tender, about 1½ hours.

Pheasant Rice Casserole

Sharon Vanderwilt, Orange City, Iowa

Ingredients:
- ¼ cup butter or margarine
- 3 cups long grain rice
- ¼ cup flour
- 1 can evaporated milk
- 1 cup pheasant broth or chicken broth
- 2½ cooked pheasants, cut into small pieces
- ½ cup water
- 1 3-oz. can sliced mushrooms
- 1½ tsp. salt
- Slivered almonds

Step 1: In saucepan, melt butter; blend in flour. Add evaporated milk, broth and water. Cook quickly, stirring constantly, until mixture thickens and bubbles. Add rice, cooked pheasant, mushrooms and salt.

Step 2: Pour into greased 2-quart casserole. Bake uncovered for 40 to 60 minutes at 350° F. Top with almonds.

Baked Pheasant and Rice

Sheryl Gallup, St. Paul, Minnesota

Ingredients:
- 2 pheasants, cut into serving-size pieces
- Salt
- Pepper
- ¼ cup butter
- 1 16-oz pkg. long grain and wild rice
- 1 cup cream of chicken soup
- ¾ cup Sauterne or other white wine
- 1 13-oz. can sliced mushrooms
- ½ cup celery, sliced
- 1 Tbsp. chopped pimento

Step 1: Season pheasant with salt and pepper to taste. Brown in butter in a skillet.

Step 2: Prepare rice according to package directions. Spoon rice into greased baking dish. Top with pheasant.

Step 3: Combine soup and remaining ingredients in saucepan. Blend well. Bring to a boil. Pour over pheasant.

Step 4: Cover and bake at 350° F. for 30 minutes. Uncover and bake an additional 15 to 20 minutes.

Iowa Hunters Help Kids with Cancer

Members of the Johnson County, Iowa, Pheasants Forever Chapter prove that hunters have heart. Several chapter members are involved with the Aiming for a Cure Foundation as board members or volunteers.

The mission of Aiming for a Cure is to raise funds to benefit pediatric oncology patients served by Children's Hospital of Iowa at the University of Iowa Hospitals and Clinics, working through the Children's Miracle Network. The goal is to improve the quality of care and quality of lives of these children and their families.

Each year, a two-day pheasant hunt is held to raise money for the foundation. Groups of hunters are matched with a celebrity, and the teams compete based on a point system. The winners are announced and several raffles are held at a banquet following the hunt.

With the help of generous donors, sponsors and hunt participants, Aiming for a Cure has successfully raised more than $190,000 in three years for Children's Hospital of Iowa, with specific gift designations to research, patient care and family support. To learn more, visit www.aimingforacure.com.

Pheasant Stuffing

Becky Randall, Aberdeen, South Dakota

Ingredients:
- 1 pkg. stuffing mix
- 1 pkg. croutons
- ½ cup butter, melted
- 1½ cups water
- 3-4 cups cooked, cubed pheasant
- ½ cup chopped onion
- ½ cup chopped celery, pre-cooked in microwave
- ¾ cup mayonnaise
- ¼ cup chopped water chestnuts
- 1½ cups milk
- 2 eggs
- 1 can cream of mushroom soup
- Grated cheese

Step 1: Combine stuffing mix, croutons, butter and water. Mix thoroughly. Press half into a 9×13-inch pan, reserving the other half.

Step 2: Combine pheasant, onion, celery, mayonnaise and water chestnuts. Spread on top of stuffing mix in pan. Top with remaining stuffing mix.

Step 3: In a small bowl, beat milk and eggs together. Pour over the stuffing.

Step 4: Cover and refrigerate overnight. (Can also freeze at this point for later use.)

Step 5: Spread mushroom soup over the dish. Bake uncovered at 325° F. for 40 minutes. Sprinkle with grated cheese and bake 10 minutes longer.

Creamed Fried Pheasant

Jeff and Rebecca Holmquist, Cokato, Minnesota

Ingredients:
- 2 whole pheasants
- 1-2 cups cream or milk
- 2-4 Tbsp. butter
- 1-2 cups flour
- Seasoned salt
- 1 large can cream of mushroom soup
- 1 small can cream of mushroom soup

Step 1: Cut pheasants into small chunks or strips, or just quarter it. Dip pieces into milk or cream, roll in flour mixed with seasoned salt, dip in milk again, then dip in seasoned flour again.

Step 2: Fry in butter until no longer pink and outside crust is crispy and golden brown.

Step 3: Place fried pheasant in a 9×13-inch glass cake pan. Pour cream of mushroom soup over the top and bake at 350° F. for 30 minutes. Serve with baked potatoes and asparagus.

> Our success can be measured not only in acres of habitat enhanced, but in relationships forged between landowners and conservationists.

Jeff Finden, PF Executive Director

Pheasant Apple Stew

Colleen Duggan, wife of Pheasants Forever VP of Corporate Relations and Marketing, and Joe Duggan, Minneapolis, Minnesota

Ingredients:

1½-2 lbs. pheasant meat
    Seasoned flour
  ¼ cup olive oil
  2 Tbsp. olive oil
  1 cup onions, chopped
  2 cups celery, chopped
    Pinch of allspice
  2 bay leaves
  2 cups carrots, cut into chunks
2-3 Macintosh or Honey Crisp apples, chopped
  1 cup dried cranberries
1½ cups apple cider
  3 cups chicken stock
  1 Tbsp. cornstarch
  1 Tbsp. water

Step 1: Cover the bottom of a heavy 4-quart saucepan with ¼ cup olive oil. Cut pheasant meat into chunks, roll in seasoned flour, and sauté until browned. Remove from pan.

Step 2: Add 2 Tbsp. olive oil to the pan. Sauté onions and celery. Add allspice, bay leaves and carrots. Cook covered 10 minutes until tender.

Step 3: Add apples, cranberries, cider and chicken stock. Cover and cook over medium heat 30 minutes.

Step 4: Mix cornstarch and water together. Stir into mixture and cook until thickened.

Sweet and Sour Pheasant

Tom and Sam (Sylvia) Kuball, Waterville, Minnesota

Ingredients:

  3 pheasant breasts, deboned
  1 cup teriyaki sauce
  2 Tbsp. olive oil
    Juice of 1 lemon, freshly squeezed
  2 cups brown rice
  2 onions
  1 green pepper
  1 red pepper
  3 large carrots
  1 cup water
  2 Tbsp. soy sauce
  3 Tbsp. honey
  ¼ cup ketchup
1½ pkg. sweet and sour seasoning mix
  1 Tbsp. cornstarch
  1 large can pineapple chunks

Step 1: Place pheasant breasts in a resealable bag. Add teriyaki sauce, olive oil and lemon juice. Refrigerate all day or overnight, turning often.

Step 2: Discard marinade. Cook pheasant until barely done, just so the pink is out of the meat. Cube cooled meat, refrigerate in covered dish.

Step 3: Cook brown rice according to directions. Set aside.

Step 4: Slice onions, peppers and carrots into large chunks; place in a large Dutch oven or kettle. Add water and cook just until done. Add soy sauce, honey, ketchup and seasoning mix. Sprinkle cornstarch over the top and fold mixture together. Heat until thickened on medium-low heat.

Step 5: Add pheasant cubes and pineapple, drained slightly. Heat until warmed through. Serve over rice.

Pheasant Casserole

Cara Waller, Ottumwa, Iowa

Ingredients:
- 1 6-oz. pkg. dry bread stuffing mix
- 4 Tbsp. butter, melted
- 1½ cups hot water
- 1 10.5-oz. can chicken gravy
- 1 lb. cooked pheasant, cubed
- 1 16-oz. pkg. frozen mixed vegetables
- ½ cup sweet onion, chopped
- ½ cup celery, chopped
- ¼ tsp. lemon pepper
- ¼ tsp. minced garlic
- ¼ tsp. salt
- ¼ tsp. pepper

Step 1: In a large bowl, combine the seasoning packet from the stuffing mix with the butter and water. Stir in the stuffing crumbs until all the liquid is absorbed.

Step 2: In a separate 2-quart casserole dish, combine the gravy, pheasant, onion, celery, vegetables and seasonings. Stir until combined.

Step 3: Spoon the stuffing mix over the top of the pheasant mixture. Bake at 350° F. for 45 minutes, or until hot and bubbly.

9-to-5 Pheasant

Dean Turek, Pheasants Forever Chapter 821 Habitat Chair, Rice County, Minnesota

Ingredients:
- 2-4 pheasant breasts
- 1 can cream of chicken soup
- White rice
- 6-12 slices thick bacon
- 1 cup milk

Step 1: Wrap bacon around pheasant breasts. Pour soup into slow cooker and place bacon-wrapped breasts on top. Cook on low for at least 8 hours.

Step 2: In the last hour of cooking, add milk to slow cooker. Serve over rice.

Nice Weather for a Hunt

Matt Kucharski, marketing/PR adviser for PF/QF National, Maple Grove, Minnesota

We've all seen a lot of things while hunting, but until last fall, I'd never hunted in a tornado. I was invited to the Pheasants Forever board of directors meeting in September of 2007 in South Dakota to train the board on effective media relations. It just so happened that it was also early goose season in the state.

We couldn't pass that up, so despite temperatures in the high 80s and humidity that felt more like Florida, a few of us enlisted a local guide and set up layout blinds and decoys on the downside of a cut cornfield. For about an hour, we sat there, without a bird in the sky — not a goose, not a pheasant, not even a sparrow. Then, about 10 miles off to the west, we noticed some clouds building ... and build-ing ... and building. Pretty soon, one of the guys said, "Hey, I've

never seen one before, but isn't that a funnel cloud?" Then another guy said, "Yeah, I think so, and isn't that a wall cloud over there?" Then a third guy said, "Hey, isn't that a tornado over there?"

After about five minutes of debate, we decided the best thing to do was to sit tight, in our layout blinds, and wait it out — figuring that any attempt to get to safer ground would have a reverse effect. We watched the whole system pass through about five miles away from us, hunted the rest of the evening, and then went back to the lodge to tell our story.

The guys back at the lodge were relieved to see that we were OK. While we had a great story to tell, I mentioned that we were disappointed that we didn't get any geese. To that, Howard Vincent replied, "Well, of course not, you idiot. Even a goose knows enough not to go out in a tornado!"

Pheasant Noodle Soup

Dean Turek, Pheasants Forever Chapter 821 Habitat Chair, Rice County, Minnesota

Ingredients:
- 1-2 pheasant breasts, cut into bite-size pieces
- 1 qt. chicken broth
- 1 Tbsp. cornstarch or flour
- 1 cup carrots, chopped
- 1 cup celery, chopped
- ¼ cup onions, diced
- Pinch of parsley
- Salt
- Pepper
- 2 cups uncooked noodles

Step 1: Whisk broth and starch together and place into slow cooker. Add remaining ingredients except noodles. Cook on low for 8 to 10 hours.

Step 2: 20 minutes before serving, cook noodles and add to slow cooker.

Pheasant Stew with Dumplings

Sheila Sandness, Bismarck, North Dakota

Ingredients:
- 3 pheasant breasts, cut into bite-size pieces
- 1 Tbsp. butter
- Nonstick spray
- 1 cup flour
- 1 tsp. salt
- 1 tsp. pepper
- 4 carrots, peeled and diced
- 1 cup celery, diced
- 1 onion, diced
- 1 14 oz. can Italian herb seasoned chicken broth
- 1 14-oz. can plain chicken broth
- 1 can cream of chicken soup
- 1¼ cups baking mix
- ½ cup milk

Step 1: Combine flour, salt and pepper in shallow dish. Coat pheasant pieces in mixture. Heat butter and nonstick spray in large frying pan with high sides and lid. Brown pheasant.

Step 2: Add carrots, celery and onion to pan, and cook for a few minutes. Add broths and soup. Cover and simmer until pheasant is fully cooked.

Step 3: Combine baking mix and milk; drop by small spoonfuls on top of stew. Cook uncovered 10 minutes. Cover and cook 10 minutes more.

Pheasant Stew

Sharon Vanderwilt, Orange City, Iowa

Ingredients:
- 1-2 pheasants
- 9 pieces bacon
- 4 onions, chopped
- 2 cans cream of potato soup
- 1 pint half and half
- 1 cup uncooked wild rice
- 1 cup Velveeta cheese

Step 1: Cook pheasants in water for about one hour or until done. Cut off bone and cube.

Step 2: Sauté bacon with onions.

Step 3: Cook wild rice according to package directions.

Step 4: Add all ingredients to slow cooker and cook for several hours until cheese is melted and dish is heated through. Serve in pastry shells or over biscuits.

Pheasant Wild Rice Soup

Sheila Sandness, Bismarck, North Dakota

Ingredients:
- 1 cup wild rice
- 6 cups water
- 5 chicken bouillon cubes
- 1 cup diced carrots
- 1 cup diced celery
- 6-8 pheasant breasts, finely diced
- 2 10-oz. cans cream of chicken soup
- 1-2 soup cans of milk

Step 1: Boil wild rice in water and bouillon cubes until it pops open. This can take up to an hour or more.

Step 2: Add diced carrots, celery, and pheasant. Cook until tender.

Step 3: Add cream of chicken soup and enough milk to achieve to desired consistency. Heat through and serve.

Although wives might favor blue jeans and sweatshirts over the skins of wild animals worn by our foremothers, seeing a husband trudge to the door with a full day's beard and a bird in each hand is delightfully primeval. He might not be Kevin Costner at the door, but it does mean something to be married to a man who dances with pheasants.

Carole Achterhof, Spirit Lake, Iowa

Pheasant Soup with Rice

Tim Fribley, Marion County Pheasants Forever, Pella, Iowa

Ingredients:
- 4 cups water
- 5 chicken bouillon cubes
- 1 large bag frozen peas and carrots
- 2 tsp. parsley flakes
- ½ tsp. seasoning salt
- 2 pheasants, cut into 1-inch cubes
- 1 box wild rice (non-instant type)

Step 1: Apply garlic and basil to taste to pheasant pieces. Seal in plastic storage bag and marinate overnight in refrigerator.

Step 2: In medium saucepan, combine water and chicken bouillon cubes. Bring to a boil and stir until bouillon is dissolved. Pour into slow cooker.

Step 3: Add frozen vegetables, parsley, seasoning salt and pheasant to slow cooker. Cook on lowest setting for 6 to 8 hours. One hour before serving, add unprepared rice and turn slow cooker to high setting. Serves 4.

White Chili

Rod Jonas, Dakota Pheasants Forever, Bismarck, North Dakota

Ingredients:
- 2 lbs. ground pheasant
- 1 lb. port sausage
- 1 cup onion, chopped
- 1 red bell pepper, chopped
- 1 cup chopped celery
- 1 can cream of celery soup
- 1 can cream of chicken soup
- 4 cups chicken broth
- 4 cans Great Northern beans (drained)
- 1 Tbsp. parsley
- 1 Tbsp. chili powder
- 1 Tbsp. cayenne pepper (or ½ Tbsp. for milder chili)
- 1 Tbsp. cumin
- 1½ tsp. garlic powder
- 1 8-oz. carton sour cream

Step 1: Combine ground pheasant and sausage in Dutch oven and brown until done.

Step 2: Add remaining ingredients except sour cream. Simmer about 1 hour.

Step 3: Add sour cream before serving.

Pheasant Mulligan with Dumplings

Bryan J. Van Deun, Pheasants Forever Vice President of Development, St. Paul, Minnesota

Ingredients:

- 2 pheasants, skinned and cut into serving-sized pieces
- 2 carrots, diced
- 1 onion, diced
- 2 cups potatoes, diced
- 1 cup cabbage, finely shredded
- 2 Tbsp. bacon drippings
- Salt
- Pepper
- Sage
- 2 cups flour, sifted
- 4 tsp. baking powder
- 2 tsp. salt
- 1 egg
- ¾ cup milk

Step 1: Cover pheasant pieces with water and cook in large Dutch oven or deep kettle.

Step 2: 30 minutes before pheasant is done, add carrots, onions, cabbage, potatoes and bacon drippings. Add salt, pepper and sage to taste. Cook until meat and vegetables are tender.

Step 3: Sift flour, baking powder and 2 tsp. salt together. Beat egg and add milk to egg. Stir into dry ingredients, adding milk as necessary to form drop-batter consistency.

Step 4: Drop batter with a tablespoon into stew and cover. Cook 15 minutes without lifting lid. Serve from kettle.

Pheasant Gumbo

Mark and Jennifer Tobin, Burt County PF Chapter, Blair, Nebraska

Ingredients:

- 1 Tbsp. olive oil
- 1 cup pheasant breast halves, chopped
- 1 lb. smoked pork sausage, thinly sliced
- 1 cup olive oil
- 1 cup all-purpose flour
- 4 tsp. minced garlic
- 3 qts. chicken broth
- 1 12-oz. can or bottle beer
- 6 stalks celery, diced
- 4 Roma (plum) tomatoes, diced
- 1 sweet onion, sliced
- 2 10-oz. cans diced tomatoes with green chili peppers, with liquid
- 2 Tbsp. chopped fresh red chili peppers
- ⅔ cup Cajun seasoning
- 1 lb. shrimp, peeled and deveined

Step 1: Heat oil in a medium skillet over medium-high heat, and cook pheasant until no longer pink and juices run clear. Stir in sausage, and cook until evenly browned. Drain pheasant and sausage, and set aside.

Step 2: In a large, heavy saucepan over medium heat, blend olive oil and flour to create a roux. Stir constantly until browned and bubbly. Mix in garlic, and cook about 1 minute.

Step 3: Gradually stir chicken broth and beer into the roux mixture. Bring to a boil, and mix in celery, tomatoes, sweet onion, diced tomatoes with green chili peppers, red chili peppers, parsley and Cajun seasoning. Reduce heat, cover, and simmer about 40 minutes, stirring often.

Step 4: Mix pheasant, sausage and shrimp into the broth mixture. Cook, stirring frequently, about 20 minutes. Serve over steamed rice.

Yogurt Marinade for Turkey or Pheasant

Sheryl Gallup, St. Paul, Minnesota

Ingredients:
- 6 Tbsp. extra virgin olive oil
- 1 Tbsp. soy sauce
- 3 Tbsp. lemon juice
- 2 Tbsp. beef bouillon powder
- 1 tsp. salt
- ¼ tsp. freshly ground black pepper
- ¼ tsp. nutmeg
- ¼ tsp. cinnamon
- 1 cup plain yogurt
- Pinch of saffron (optional)

Step 1: Mix all ingredients in a glass bowl or pan. Add meat and stir until covered with marinade. Cover and refrigerate overnight, turning meat several times.

Step 2: Grill meat until done. You can pour excess marinade on meat at the beginning of the cooking process, but do not baste throughout grilling process.

Pheasant Chowder

Becky Randall, Aberdeen, South Dakota

Ingredients:
- 2 cups carrots, sliced
- 8-10 slices bacon, roughly chopped
- 2 cups celery, diced
- 1 cup onion, diced
- 1 tsp. garlic, minced
- 3-4 potatoes, cooked
- 3 qts. chicken stock
- 2 pints cream
- 3-5 skinless pheasants, boiled (can also use chicken breasts)
- Roux (equal parts flour and butter)*

Step 1: In a large saucepan, combine cream and chicken stock; warm to a medium boil. Add roux to thicken. Finish with salt and pepper to taste.

Step 2: Cook bacon until brown and add to cream sauce.

Step 3: Add vegetables and garlic to the hot pan with the bacon grease. When the onions become slightly tender, add the vegetables to the cream sauce.

Step 4: Dice and cook pheasant or chicken and season to taste. Add chicken to saucepan. Add cooked potatoes. Let simmer add salt and pepper if needed.

*Note: To make roux, melt butter in a heavy skillet over medium-low heat. Stir in flour, a little at a time, with a wooden spoon. Cook, stirring constantly, until the mixture turns light brown.

Whiskey Marinade

Kirk Augustine, Omaha, Nebraska
This recipe will easily marinade eight 14-ounce filets, six to eight 12-ounce ribeyes, or 1 to 2 pounds of finger-size pheasant pieces.

Ingredients:
- 2 Tbsp. olive oil
- 2 Tbsp. Worchestershire sauce
- 1-2 tsp. garlic powder
- ½ tsp. onion powder
- 1-2 tsp. black pepper
- 2-3 drops Liquid Smoke
- 4-6 oz. Southern Comfort
- 8-12 oz. soy sauce
- 8-12 oz. Diet Coke (Coca-Cola brand only)

Step 1: In a 16- to 20-ounce vessel, combine all ingredients except Diet Coke. Stir to completely combine.

Step 2: Immediately before applying to meat, add Diet Coke and stir. Place marinade in resealable plastic bag. Add meat of your choice and seal.

Step 3: While the grill or fryer is heating up, turn the bag every five to 10 minutes to coat every surface. Avoid leaving the meat pieces in the marinade over 30 minutes or the marinade will overpower the meat flavors.

Step 4: Grill steaks or deep fry pheasant pieces for 1 to 3 minutes until done.

Fish and Game Fry Batter

Retired Minnesota State Senator Bob Lessard
Lessard's wildlife legislation included Minnesota's Constitutional Right to Hunt and Fish, and the creation of Minnesota's Hunting Heritage Week.

Ingredients:
- 1 cup flour
- 1 tsp. salt
- 1 tsp. garlic salt
- ½ tsp. black pepper
- 1 tsp. baking powder
- Pinch of dill weed
- 1 cup beer, flat
- 1 egg

Step 1: Combine all dry ingredients. In a separate bowl, mix egg and beer. Pour liquid ingredients into flour mixture and stir. Add more beer or flour as needed to thin or thicken mixture.

Step 2: Pat fish, pheasant or other game dry with paper towels. Dip in batter and fry in oil until golden brown. The oil should be hot enough that the battered meat rises to the top immediately.

Note: When doubling this recipe, double all ingredients and add an extra egg. Recipe can be used for onion rings and chicken as well.

Pheasant-Wrapped Jalapeño Poppers

Dustin Schirm, Prairie Creek PF Chapter of Benton County, Garrison, Iowa

Ingredients:
- 1 pheasant breast
- 3 whole jalapeño peppers, fresh or canned
- ½ cup cream cheese
- 6 bacon slices
- Salt
- Pepper
- 1 cup teriyaki sauce

Step 1: Cut the meat off the breast, and filet meat as thinly as possible, into 6 slices. Set aside.

Step 2: Cut jalapeño peppers in half, remove seeds, and fill with cream cheese.

Step 3: Place filled pepper half on a piece of filleted pheasant and roll up. Wrap bacon strip around the outside, secure with toothpick, and salt and pepper to taste.

Step 4: Marinate poppers in teriyaki sauce for 2 to 4 hours. Discard marinade and grill until meat is done.

Lemon Pheasant Fingers

Ron Schara, host of "Minnesota Bound" television show, and Chef John Schumacher

Ingredients:
- 4 pheasant breasts, boneless, skinless
- 8 eggs
- ¾ cup Parmesan cheese
- ⅓ cup butter, clarified
- 1 cup seasoned flour
- 2 cups bread crumbs
- 1 Tbsp. fresh lemon juice
- 2 tsp. lemon pepper seasoning
- Salt and pepper to taste.

Step 1: Remove skin and silver skin from pheasant breasts and slice each breast into six strips about the size of a forefinger.

Step 2: Combine eggs and Parmesan cheese and beat to a smooth consistency. Heat butter in a large sauté pan.

Step 3: Dredge pheasant fingers in flour, dip into egg batter, and roll in bread crumbs. Sauté in butter until golden brown. Splash with lemon juice. Season with lemon pepper, salt and pepper.

Step 4: Turn down heat and cook for 3 minutes, turning meat to keep from over-browning. Serve the fingers with assorted sauces.

Note: A whole skinless, boneless breast can be prepared in the same way, but finish in a 350° F. oven for 20 minutes. Serves 4.

Grilled Pheasant Appetizers

Randy Johnson, Cass County PF Chapter 660, Ralston, Nebraska

Ingredients:

- Pheasant, deboned and cut into 1-inch chunks (can also use turkey)
- 1 large green pepper, cut into 1- to 2-inch pieces
- 1 medium red onion, cut into 1- to 2-inch pieces
- 1 medium bottle Italian dressing, oil based
- 1 pkg. bacon, preferably maple cured
- Crushed black pepper

Step 1: Place cut up bird, peppers and onions in a large resealable plastic bag. Add dressing, shake to coat, and store in refrigerator several hours or until ready to grill, turning frequently.

Step 2: Wrap each slice of bacon around one piece each of the meat, onion and green pepper. Secure with toothpick. Season with black pepper.

Step 3: Grill appetizers over low heat until the bacon is cooked and dark brown.

Maple-Chili Grilled Quail

John Linquist, Pheasants Forever regional representative, Sibley, Iowa

Ingredients:

- 8 quail, semi-boneless
- ½ cup pure maple syrup
- 2 Tbsp. pure chili powder
- 2 Tbsp. vegetable oil
- Salt
- Freshly ground pepper

Step 1: Light a grill or preheat the broiler.

Step 2: In a small bowl, combine the maple syrup and chili powder.

Step 3: Brush the quail with the oil and season with salt and pepper. Grill or broil on a rimmed baking sheet until browned, about 1 minute per side.

Step 4: Use a brush to coat the quail with the maple glaze. Grill or broil them, breast side toward the heat, for about 2 minutes, or until the quail are well browned and just pink at the bone. Serves 8.

Goose or Duck Pâté

Bill Stevens, Anoka, Minnesota
My wife is not fond of duck, goose or woodcock because the meat has a strong flavor. I tried various recipes and finally found one that she would eat. Many hunters don't keep the legs of geese, and I have always been willing to give them a temporary home in my freezer — at least until the Christmas holidays.

Ingredients:
- 6 cups duck and/or goose meat
- Onions, peppers, celery, garlic, bay leaf, salt, pepper or spices of your choice
- 1½ cups onion, chopped
- 6 garlic cloves, chopped
- 3 Tbsp. mayonnaise
- Tabasco sauce to taste
- 2 Tbsp. basil, finely chopped
- 18 oz. cream cheese
- Salt
- Pepper

Step 1: To cook the meat, boil in water with vegetables and spices of your choice. Drain, reserve vegetables, and remove meat from bones.

Step 2: Grind together the cooked meat, vegetables used to cook the meat (remove bay leaf, if used), onions and garlic. Place mixture in a large mixing bowl.

Step 3: Add mayonnaise, salt, pepper, basil and cream cheese. Refrigerate overnight, or freeze and use within 2 to 3 months.

Saskatchewan Baked Partridge

Paul Hanson, Past Chair and Current Board Member
PF National Board, Sauk Rapids, Minnesota

Ingredients:
- 4 partridge
- Seasoned flour
- 1 can cream of mushroom soup
- 1 cup vegetable oil
- 2 bay leaves
- 4 medium-size potatoes
- 8 carrots
- 2 cups fresh mushrooms
- ⅓ cup cream sherry
- ⅓ cup white wine

Step 1: Clean partridge and cut in half. Dredge in seasoned flour. Heat oil and brown partridge.

Step 2: Place birds in a large casserole. Add chicken stock, bay leaves, cream of mushroom soup and one can of water. Cover tightly and bake for one hour at 350° F.

Step 3: Peel and cut potatoes in half. Peel and cut carrots into 4-inch slices. Cut onions into ½-inch slices. Wash and quarter mushrooms.

Step 4: Add vegetables, cream sherry, white wine and salt to partridge and bake an additional hour at 350° F. or until carrots and potatoes are tender. Remove bay leaves and serve. Serves 4.

Alfredo Tomato Duck with Pasta

Don Bergler, Winona, Minnesota

Ingredients:

- 3-4 mallard breasts or 5-6 bluebill breasts (can also use pheasant)
- 2 12 oz. cans Coca-Cola
- 6-8 cloves garlic, crushed
- 1 medium-large onion, chopped medium to fine
- Extra virgin olive oil
- 1 lb. jar store-bought Alfredo sauce, regular or reduced-fat
- 1 14-15 oz. can diced tomatoes with green chilies or herbs
- Mushrooms to taste
- ½ bag frozen cut green beans, or equivalent amount of fresh
- Spinach noodles
- Parmesan cheese
- Cracked black pepper

Step 1: Fillet duck from breasts and slice into ½-inch strips across the grain of the fillet. Marinate in Coca-Cola for 24 to 48 hours in the refrigerator. (If using pheasant instead of duck, skip this step.)

Step 2: Sauté garlic and onion in extra virgin olive oil. Remove from oil and set aside.

Step 3: Remove duck strips from marinade and brown in the olive oil. Add more oil if needed. Remove any remaining oil once meat is browned.

Step 4: Add garlic and onion back into the pan with the meat. Add Alfredo sauce and diced tomatoes. Add a small amount of water to the pan.

Step 5: Add thawed green beans and mushrooms (sauté first if using fresh). Simmer to heat through and cook the green beans.

Step 6: Meanwhile, prepare spinach noodles.

Step 7: Serve sauce over spinach noodles. Top with grated Parmesan and cracked black pepper.

> The ringneck pheasant is as synonymous to South Dakota as a banana is to a banana split. No other bird its size can rise as quickly and leave the most experienced hunter baffled and holding an empty gun.

Ed Carlson of Phoenix, Arizona, formerly of Columbia, South Dakota

Polynesian Wild Turkey

Carter Stults, President, Nemaha Valley, Nebraska PF Chapter; Treasurer, Nebraska State Council

Ingredients:

- 1 wild turkey breast
- 2 cups soy sauce
- 1 cup of fresh pineapple, diced or 20-oz. can crushed pineapple
- ½ cup chopped macadamia nuts, walnuts or peanuts
- 2 Tbsp. cider vinegar
- 1 tsp. salt
- 1 tsp. pepper
- 1 clove garlic
- 1 tsp. ginger
- ¼ cup olive or peanut oil

Step 1: Cut turkey breast into ½-inch strips lengthwise with the grain of the meat. Using a meat tenderizer or rolling pin, gently pound out the strips until they are generally flat.

Step 2: In a medium-size bowl, mix remaining ingredients until well blended to create marinade. In a shallow baking dish, marinate turkey strips overnight in refrigerator.

Step 3: Remove strips and discard marinade. Grill turkey breasts on medium heat until done. If you wish, baste with a mixture of soy sauce and pineapple juice during grilling. For a true Polynesian dish, serve over long grain rice with roasted sweet potatoes.

Smoked Boneless Turkey Breast

Dean Turek, Pheasants Forever Chapter 821 Habitat Chair, Rice County, Minnesota

Ingredients:

- 1 3-lb. turkey breast roll, boneless
- ½ cup coarse salt
- 2 Tbsp. brown sugar, packed
- 1 tsp. fresh thyme, finely chopped Additional thyme for smoking

Step 1: Mix salt, brown sugar and 1 teaspoon thyme.

Step 2: Cut the string holding the turkey roll, unroll and pat dry. Spread half of mixed ingredients in the roll and retie. Place roll on a glass or ceramic tray and rub the remaining mixture on top. Cover and refrigerate overnight.

Step 3: Remove meat from tray, rinse well and pat dry. Let stand for 1 to 2 hours.

Step 4: Preheat smoker to 220° F. Rub the roast rack with oil and additional chopped fresh thyme. Place meat on oiled rack and smoke for 2 to 5 hours, or until internal temperature reaches 140° F. Cooking times will vary depending on wind and weather conditions.

Stuffed Turkey Roll

Dean Turek, Pheasants Forever Chapter 821 Habitat Chair, Rice County, Minnesota

Ingredients:
- 2 lbs. boneless turkey breast
- 2 cups fresh mushrooms, sliced
- 3 green onions, finely chopped
- 1 medium carrot, finely chopped
- 1 stalk celery, finely sliced
- 2 Tbsp. butter
  Salt
  Pepper
  Poultry seasoning
  Chicken broth
- 1 Tbsp. fresh lemon juice
- 2 slices bread, cubed
- 1 medium tomato, seeded and diced

Step 1: Butterfly the turkey and use a meat tenderizer to pound thin.

Step 2: Sauté mushrooms, onions, carrot and celery in butter.

Step 3: Mix together the bread, tomatoes and sauteed vegetables. Add lemon juice and enough chicken broth to make the mixture moist. Add salt, pepper and poultry seasoning to taste.

Step 4: Spread stuffing mixture over butterflied meat. Roll up and tie well. Rub outside with additional juice.

Step 5: Preheat smoker to 120° to 220° F. Place turkey roll on an oiled rack in the upper half of the smoker. Smoke cook for 5 to 6 hours, or until the internal temperature reaches 160° F. Cooking times will vary depending on wind and weather conditions. Serve with cranberry sauce, mashed potatoes and gravy.

Rabbit in Brown Sauce

John Linquist, Pheasants Forever Regional Representative, Sibley, Iowa

Ingredients:
- 1 rabbit
- 2 oz. butter
- ¼ lb. bacon
  Pepper to taste
- 6 green onions
- ¾ oz. flour
- 1 pint brown sauce
  Fresh button mushrooms

Step 1: Clean rabbit and cut into quarters.

Step 2: Melt butter in skillet and fry rabbit for 5 minutes. Dice uncooked bacon and add to skillet with rabbit. Add pepper and sliced onions. Fry 10 minutes longer.

Step 3: Sprinkle flour over ingredients. Add brown sauce and simmer gently for 1 hour. Add stock if necessary to maintain consistency.

Step 4: Remove rabbit and strain sauce. Reheat rabbit in sauce, place on a hot dish and garnish with hot button mushrooms.

Bison Chili

Prep: 20 minutes   Cook: 70 minutes

Ingredients:
- 1 pound ground bison
- 1 medium onion, chopped
- 2 14½-oz. cans diced tomatoes
- 1 15- to 16-oz. can pinto beans, rinsed and drained
- ½ cup water
- 2 to 3 tsp. chili powder
- ½ tsp. salt
- ½ tsp. ground cumin
- ½ tsp. ground black pepper
- ¼ cup snipped fresh cilantro
  Toppers, such as shredded cheddar cheese, sliced fresh or pickled jalapeno peppers, and/or dairy sour cream (optional)

Step 1: In a large skillet cook and stir bison and onion over medium heat until bison is browned and onion is tender. Stir in undrained tomatoes, beans, water, chili powder, salt, cumin and pepper. Bring to boiling; reduce heat. Simmer, covered, for 1 hour, stirring occasionally.

Step 2: Stir in cilantro. Cover and cook 10 minutes more. If desired, add toppers to each serving. Makes 4 to 6 servings.

Nutrition Facts per serving: 281 cal., 3 g total fat (1 g sat. fat), 70 mg chol., 1047 mg sodium, 31 g carbo., 7 g dietary fiber, 33 g protein.
Daily Values: 14% vit. A, 48% vit. C, 13% calcium, 30% iron.

Venison Carne Asada Minute Steaks

Matt Kucharski, marketing/PR advisor for PF/QF National, Maple Grove, Minnesota

Ingredients:
- 2 lbs. venison, backstrap or hindquarter, cut into ½-inch to ¾-inch strips
- ¼ cup fajita seasoning
- 1 large red or white onion, sliced ¼-inch thick
- 1 large green pepper, sliced ¼-inch thick
- Mushrooms, sliced (optional)
- Salt and pepper to taste
- Olive oil or olive oil nonstick spray
- Hoagie rolls or tortillas

Step 1: Place steaks in resealable plastic bag. Add fajita seasoning, coating thoroughly, and refrigerate at least 2 hours or overnight.

Step 2: Sauté onions, peppers and mushrooms until soft, but not mushy. Season with salt and pepper. Set aside.

Step 3: Remove steaks and place between two pieces of plastic wrap. Pound as thin as possible, just short of breaking. Spray steaks with olive oil and drop into hot skillet or griddle for 30 to 45 seconds per side.

Step 4: Serve with onion/pepper/mushroom mixture on hoagie rolls or with warm tortillas. Best when served hot, but can be kept warm in low-heat oven.

Buffalo Ribs

Selmer C. (Sandy) Hanson, Sauk Rapids, Minnesota

Ingredients:
- 3 lbs. buffalo short ribs
- Oil for frying
- 1 cup ketchup or barbecue sauce
- 1 onion, sliced very thin
- ¼ cup vinegar
- 3 slices lemon
- 2 Tbsp. Worcestershire sauce
- 1 Tbsp. butter
- 1 Tbsp. salt
- ⅛ tsp. allspice
- ⅛ tsp. cinnamon

Step 1: Parboil buffalo ribs, remove and pat dry. Brown on all sides in hot oil.

Step 2: Combine other ingredients in saucepan and bring to boil, stirring constantly. Reduce heat to simmer, cover and simmer about five minutes.

Step 3: Pour sauce over browned ribs and cook in an electric slow cooker on low heat at least 6 hours but preferably all day. Another method is to roast the ribs with the sauce in a covered container at 350° F. in the oven for 2 to 3 hours, or until the ribs are tender.

Bison Stroganoff

Prep: 20 minutes   Cook: 8 minutes

Ingredients:

Better Homes and Gardens®
Test Kitchen

- 1 lb. boneless bison (buffalo) sirloin steak
- 2 Tbsp. all-purpose flour
- 1 tsp. dry mustard
- ½ tsp. salt
- ⅛ tsp. ground black pepper
- 3 Tbsp. olive oil
- 8 oz. mushrooms, thinly sliced
- 1 medium onion, chopped
- 2 cloves garlic, minced
- 2 Tbsp. all-purpose flour
- 1¼ cups beef broth
- 2 Tbsp. tomato paste
- 1 8-oz. carton dairy sour cream
  Salt and ground black pepper
- 3 cups hot cooked noodles
  Fresh parsley, snipped (optional)
  Peas, steamed (optional)

Step 1: Partially freeze bison. Cut, across grain, into thin bite-size strips. In a resealable plastic bag, combine 2 tablespoons flour, mustard, salt and pepper; add beef strips, seal bag, and shake to coat.

Step 2: In an extra-large skillet, heat 2 tablespoons of the olive oil. Add bison strips; cook 2 to 3 minutes or until browned. Remove and set aside. Add remaining oil to skillet; add mushrooms, onion and garlic. Cook over medium heat, stirring frequently, until onion is tender. Sprinkle with remaining 2 tablespoons flour. Add beef broth and tomato paste. Cook and stir until thickened and bubbly.

Step 3: Return bison to skillet; cook and stir until bison is heated through. Gradually stir about ½ cup of the sauce into the sour cream; return mixture to skillet and just heat through (do not boil). Season to taste with salt and pepper. Serve over hot cooked noodles. If desired, sprinkle with parsley and serve with steamed peas. Makes 4 servings.

Nutrition Facts per serving: 573 cal., 29 g total fat (11 g sat. fat), 140 mg chol., 744 mg sodium, 44 g carbo., 3 g dietary fiber, 36 g protein.
Daily Values: 8% vit. A, 6% vit. C, 10% calcium, 34% iron.

Hunting Party Beans
Mark Holsten, Minnesota DNR Commissioner

Ingredients:
- 2 lbs. ground beef
- 2 cups chopped onion
- 1 cup chopped celery
- 1 10¾-oz. can cream of tomato soup, undiluted
- 1 6-oz. can tomato paste
- ½ cup ketchup
- 1 16-oz. can green beans, drained
- 1 17-oz. can lima beans, drained
- 1 15½-oz. can yellow wax beans, drained
- 1 15-16 oz. can chili beans, undrained
- 1 16 oz. can pork and beans, undrained
- ½ cup packed brown sugar
- 2 Tbsp. prepared yellow mustard

Step 1: In large Dutch oven, brown beef over medium-high heat. Drain fat.

Step 2: Add onion and celery. Cook until tender. Stir in tomato soup, tomato paste and ketchup. Simmer 15 to 20 minutes.

Step 3: Spoon mixture into a large roasting pan. Add remaining ingredients and stir well. Bake, uncovered, at 350° F. for 1 hour. Makes 25 servings.

Taters and Onions
Sheryl Gallup, St. Paul, Minnesota

Ingredients:
- 8 Tbsp. butter
- 3-4 medium potatoes, sliced
- 1 large onion
  - Black pepper
  - Garlic powder
  - Cayenne pepper

Step 1: Line a frying pan with aluminum foil. Add 4 tablespoons of butter, potatoes and onion. Sprinkle with black pepper, garlic powder and cayenne pepper to taste.

Step 2: Add 4 more tablespoons of butter on top. Put another sheet of aluminum foil over the top and seal tightly.

Step 3: Cook over high heat until butter starts to bubble, then lower heat to a simmer for about 1 hour.

Herb-Rubbed Bison Sirloin Tip Roast

Prep: 20 minutes   Roast: 1¼ hours   Stand: 15 minutes

Ingredients:

- 1 Tbsp. paprika
- 2 tsp. kosher salt or sea salt or 1 tsp. salt
- 1 tsp. garlic powder
- ½ tsp. dried oregano, crushed
- ½ tsp. dried thyme, crushed
- ½ tsp. ground black pepper
- ½ tsp. onion powder
- ½ tsp. cayenne pepper
- 2 Tbsp. olive oil
- 1 3-3½-lb. boneless bison sirloin tip roast
  Roasted vegetables (optional)

Step 1: In a small bowl combine paprika, salt, garlic powder, oregano, thyme, black pepper, onion powder and cayenne pepper. Stir in oil until well combined. Set aside. Trim fat from roast. Spread oil mixture over surface of meat. Place meat on a rack in a shallow roasting pan. Insert an oven-going meat thermometer into center of meat.

Step 2: Roast in a 375° F. oven for 15 minutes. Reduce oven temperature to 300° F. Roast 60 to 65 minutes more or until meat thermometer registers 140° F. Cover roast tightly with foil and let stand in pan on a wire rack for 15 minutes. The temperature of the meat after standing should be 145° F. (medium-rare). Thinly slice meat across the grain to serve. Serve with roasted vegetables, if desired. Makes 8 servings.

Nutrition Facts per serving: 229 cal., 8 g total fat (2 g sat. fat), 121 mg chol., 570 mg sodium, 1 g carbo., 0 g dietary fiber, 37 g protein.
Daily Values: 9% vit. A, 1% vit. C, 1% calcium, 30% iron.

Minnesota Potatoes
Brad Moore, Minnesota Pollution Control (MPCA)
Commissioner

Ingredients:
- 4 potatoes, peeled
- 1 yellow summer squash
- 1 yellow onion
- 2/3 stick butter
- Salt
- Pepper
- 1 cup sour cream
- 1 cup grated Parmesan cheese

Step 1: Slice potatoes, squash and onions into slices ¼-inch thick.

Step 2: Butter deep casserole dish. Add half the potatoes, then layer half the squash on top, followed by half the onion slices. Add salt and pepper to taste and dot with ⅓ stick butter. Repeat.

Step 3: Bake uncovered at 375° F. for 1 hour.

Step 4: Mix sour cream and Parmesan cheese. Spread on top of casserole. Continue baking until browned.

ON THE SIDE
Suzy's Salad
Suzy Matuska, wife of Mark Matuska, Stearns County
Pheasants Forever chapter and regional DNR Director,
New Ulm, Minnesota

Ingredients:
- 8 cups cabbage, shredded
- 2 pkg. ramen Oriental noodles with seasoning packet
- 2 cups sunflower seeds
- 2/3 cup oil
- 3 Tbsp. sugar
- 6 Tbsp. vinegar
- Salt
- Pepper

Step 1: Break up noodles and add to large bowl. Add cabbage and sunflower seeds. Combine well.

Step 2: In a separate bowl, beat together oil, sugar, vinegar, seasoning packet, and salt and pepper to taste. Allow to stand overnight at room temperature, or 4 to 5 hours in the refrigerator.

Step 3: Pour dressing over cabbage mixture immediately before serving. Toss well to coat.

The Eastern Midwest

In this neck of the woods (and in every neck of every woods), hunters and outdoor enthusiasts owe a debt of gratitude to Aldo Leopold, known as the father of wildlife management and one of the foremost American conservationists. He also appreciated a good meal. Aldo Leopold purchased a worn-out farm in Wisconsin in 1935, and set to restoring an old chicken

coop into a family cabin affectionately called "The Shack." This is where he kept his journal and recorded seasonal observations that became his renowned book, *A Sand County Almanac*.

Leopold and his wife Estella had five children: Starker, Luna, Nina, Carl and Estella. Nina Leopold Bradley (bottom right), who lives near The Shack outside Baraboo, shared this story and recipe from her childhood.

Weekends at The Shack

Nina Leopold Bradley, Baraboo, Wisconsin
Weekends at the Leopold Shack were delightful times of work, play, exploration and camaraderie. Appetites increased with the level of activity. Breakfast became a major meal and sourdough pancakes helped accommodate very large appetites. On occasion, eating pancakes became a contest as to who, of the five of us teenagers, could eat the most pancakes. Luna became the family champion one morning when he devoured twelve sourdough pancakes.

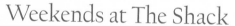

Sourdough Pancakes, Aldo Leopold Style

In the evening, before the music begins (guitar and singing in front of the fire), mix the sourdough batter for the morning breakfast. This amount is for about six people. For more people, add more water and flour.

Ingredients:
- 1 Tbsp. yeast or one package of yeast
- Flour
- 1-3 eggs
- 1-3 Tbsp. sugar or honey
- ½ tsp. salt
- 1 tsp. soda

Step 1: Dissolve yeast in one to two cups of lukewarm water and add flour until it is the consistency of a thick batter. Cover and keep warm during the night.

Step 2: In the morning, add eggs, sugar or honey, salt and soda. Stir well and pour individual servings into a hot frying pan or Dutch oven. Roll around to produce a thin pancake the size of the pan. As the batter begins to bubble and the under surface becomes brown, turn and cook until the second side is brown. Serve on a hot plate. Apply butter and syrup and roll the pancake into a kind of jellyroll.

Step 3: Keep and cover any remaining dough. The next evening, repeat the process, adding flour and water for the amount needed for the next morning. Repeat as desired.

Smoked Pheasant Log

Jim Bourcier, Midland, Michigan

Ingredients:
- 1 smoked pheasant breast (or 1 cooked breast and ¼ tsp. liquid smoke)
- 1 8-oz. pkg. cream cheese, softened
- 2 Tbsp. onion, grated
- 1 Tbsp. lemon juice
- 1 tsp. prepared horseradish
- ¼ tsp. salt
- ½ cup parsley, chopped
- ½ cup pecans, chopped

Step 1: Cook breast with liquid smoke if not smoked. Shred meat in blender or processor.

Step 2: Combine all ingredients except parsley and pecans. Shape into a log. Wrap in aluminum foil and chill.

Step 3: Roll log in parsley and pecans before serving with crackers or breadsticks.

Pheasant Cordon Bleu

Kraig Shafer, Pheasants Forever Chapter 260, Cairo, Ohio

Ingredients:
- 4 pheasant breasts
- 16 ham slices, very thinly sliced
- 4 Swiss or Cheddar cheese slices, sliced thick
- 2 cups cracker crumbs
- 1 tsp. garlic salt
- Cajun seasoning to taste

Step 1: Filet 4 pheasant breasts so you have 8 boneless filets. Stay next to the bone when you're cutting so you have nice thick filets. Slit about ¾ of the way through each filet to form a pocket in each piece.

Step 2: Stuff each pocket with two slices of ham and a slice of Swiss or Cheddar cheese. Fold the pocket shut and run a toothpick through the meat to hold it shut.

Step 3: Roll each stuffed filet in cracker crumbs seasoned with garlic salt and Cajun seasoning.

Step 4: Brown the filets in a greased skillet just until they are lightly browned, then arrange them on a greased baking dish and bake at 350° F. for 45 minutes. Don't overcook.

Serve with grilled asparagus and mashed potatoes. Put some pheasant gravy over the whole thing and enjoy!

Smoked Bacon-Wrapped Pheasant

Terry McNalley, Williams County Chapter 283, Bryan, Ohio

Ingredients:
- 1 pheasant breast fillet
- 4 cups water
- ½ cup Tender Quick salt
- ½ cup Worcestershire sauce
- ½ cup brown sugar
- ¼ tsp. coarse pepper
- ½ lb. bacon

Step 1: Cut pheasant into ½-inch strips.

Step 2: Place all ingredients into a large plastic storage bag along with pheasant. Marinate in refrigerator 8 hours, turning frequently.

Step 3: Remove pheasant from bag, pat dry. Roll and wrap each piece with a half slice of bacon.

Step 4: Place in smoker at 160° F. for 1½ to 2 hours or until done. Check frequently. Mesquite or any flavored chips may be used. Serve as an hors d'oeuvre or appetizer.

Maple Pheasant with Bacon

Doug Burrows, Eau Claire, Wisconsin

Ingredients:
- Pheasant breasts
- Apple- or maple-cured bacon slices, thick-cut
- ⅔ cup maple syrup
- ⅔ cup soy sauce
- ½ cup brown sugar
- Splash of Worcestershire sauce
- Garlic powder
- Onion powder
- Pepper
- Celery salt

Step 1: Filet breast off the bone and wrap each piece with bacon.

Step 2: Combine remaining ingredients and pour over bacon-wrapped pheasant breasts. Cover and marinate in refrigerator overnight.

Step 3: Place pheasant in baking dish. Cover with some of the marinade. Discard remaining marinade. Cover baking dish with foil. Bake at 350° F. for 1 hour, then uncover and bake another ½ hour.

Too Shocked to Shoot

Jim Simpson, Tippe River Basin, Indiana, Pheasants Forever Chapter 533

While hunting with my two teenage sons, we were walking a fence line and not having much action. I told my boys that pheasants like to sit next to fence posts and hide. Getting the, "Yeah right, Dad" look, they grabbed the next fence post they walked by and a hen flew up right in front of both of them. Good thing it was a hen because they were too surprised to shoot!

Pheasant Pot Pie

Mary Engel, Frankenmuth, Michigan

Ingredients:
- Pastry for two-crust deep-dish pie
- 2 Tbsp. butter
- 1 cup carrots, chopped
- 1½ cups celery, chopped
- 2 cups fresh mushrooms, sliced
- ½ cup onion, chopped
- 1 cup frozen peas
- 2 cups pheasant, cooked and diced
- 1 tsp. chicken seasoning
- Salt
- Pepper
- 2 cups chicken broth
- Cornstarch

Step 1: Sauté carrots, celery, mushrooms and onion in butter until tender.

Step 2: Cook peas until slightly firm and add to pan.

Step 3: Add cooked pheasant and chicken seasoning, plus salt and pepper to taste. Stir in chicken broth. Thicken with cornstarch to desired consistency.

Step 4: Pour into pastry-lined pan. Cover with the second pie crust. Bake 30 to 40 minutes at 425° F. until golden brown.

Pheasant Stir-Fry

Dorothy Zehnder, Frankenmuth, Michigan

Ingredients:
- 2 Tbsp. soy sauce
- 1 Tbsp. fresh ginger root, minced, or ¾ tsp. ground ginger
- 1 Tbsp. chicken bouillon granules
- 1⅓ cup water
- 1 boneless skinless pheasant breast (about ¾ pound)
- 1 cup broccoli florets
- 2 Tbsp. cornstarch
- 1 cup carrots, julienned
- 1 cup celery, julienned
- 1 cup onion, julienned
- 1 cup frozen snow peas
- Hot cooked white or wild rice
- Cooking oil

Step 1: In a small bowl, combine soy sauce, cornstarch, ginger, bouillon and water. Set aside. (If desired, use 1¾ cups unsalted chicken broth, seasoned to taste, in place of bouillon and water.)

Step 2: Cut pheasant into strips. In a skillet or wok over medium-high heat, stir-fry pheasant in 1 tablespoon of oil until no longer pink, about 3 to 4 minutes. Remove and keep warm.

Step 3: Add more oil to pan. Stir-fry broccoli and carrots for 2 minutes. Add celery, onion and peas. Stir-fry until all vegetables are crisp-tender, about 4 to 5 minutes.

Step 4: Stir soy sauce mixture and add to skillet; bring to a boil. Cook and stir 2 more minutes. Return meat to pan and heat through. Serve over rice. Serves 4.

February Pheasant

Robert Shields, Bucyrus, Ohio

Ingredients:

(Use whatever quantities you have available.)

Pheasant quarter sections, deboned except leg

Stanley Island seasoning

Flour

Olive oil

Shallots

Pheasant stock

Rosemary

Heavy cream

Shiitake mushrooms

Step 1: Season flour with Stanley Island seasoning. Dredge pheasant quarters in seasoned flour, tapping off excess flour.

Step 2: Quickly brown pheasant quarters in olive oil. Remove from pan and set aside.

Step 3: Caramelize shallots in pan. De-glaze pan with pheasant stock. Add a pinch of rosemary. Simmer until stock is reduced by two-thirds.

Step 4: Add heavy cream. Simmer until reduced by half.

Step 5: Add shiitake mushrooms, stir and simmer 1 minute more.

Step 6: Place pheasant back into pan with sauce. Cover and roast 25 minutes until juice runs clear. Do not overcook.

Step 7: Place pheasant onto plate, spoon mushroom cream sauce over top. Garnish with fresh rosemary sprig. Serve with wild rice and fresh asparagus.

Pheasant Oscar

Tim Wendt, Cross Plains, Wisconsin

Ingredients:

2 pheasant breasts

Seasoning salt

1 bunch asparagus

4 oz. hollandaise sauce, homemade or prepared from mix

Snow crab claws or canned crab meat

Step 1: Season breasts with seasoning salt. Sauté or grill to your liking.

Step 2: Cook asparagus until tender. Place asparagus on serving plate with the cooked breasts and top with hollandaise sauce. Garnish with heated crab claws or meat.

Roast Pheasant with Apple Walnut Stuffing and Gravy

Tim Wendt, Cross Plains, Wisconsin

Ingredients:

- 2 whole pheasants
- ¼ stick butter
- 4 cups cubed day old bread, toasted
- 4 cups seasoned croutons
- 2 Granny Smith apples, cored and diced
- 1 yellow onion, chopped
- 1 cup celery, chopped
- ½ cup walnuts
- 2 10-oz. cans chicken stock
- Sage
- Rosemary leaves
- Thyme leaves
- Seasoning salt
- Black pepper
- 3 Tbsp. cornstarch

Step 1: Heat oven to 350° F. Melt butter in a 10-inch skillet. Add onion, celery and apples. Cook until tender.

Step 2: Add one can of chicken stock to skillet. Simmer for 5 minutes.

Step 3: Mix contents of pan with bread, croutons and walnuts.

Step 4: Stuff pheasants with mixture. Place in a baking pan and season birds with seasoning salt, black pepper, sage, rosemary and thyme. Roast 45 minutes to 1 hour or until juices run clear. Baste if necessary. If desired, birds may be wrapped in bacon or aluminum foil. If this is done, remove bacon or foil for the last 10 minutes so the birds may brown.

Step 5: When meat is done, remove birds from pan, add one can chicken stock and bring to a boil. Thicken with a mixture of cornstarch and ¼ cup cold water to make gravy.

Jean's Pheasant Casserole

This recipe is based on Jean Bush's ever-popular pheasant casserole dish, and was contributed in her memory by John and Lois Bush, Shavehead Lake, Cassopolis, Michigan.

Ingredients:
1-3 pheasants
  1 can cream soup (mushroom, chicken, celery, etc.)
  1 cup onion, chopped fine
  ½ cup celery, chopped
  2 cloves garlic, minced
    Bread crumbs
  1 cup or more grated Cheddar cheese

Step 1: Parboil pheasants until tender (falling off the bone). Cool, debone pheasant, and cut into manageable chunks.

Step 2: Mix pheasant, onion, celery and garlic together. Pour into baking dish. Pour soup on top of mixture. (If you have a lot of meat, use 2 cans of soup.)

Step 3: Top with crumbs and cheese. Bake at 350° F. for one hour or until done.

Woody's Grilled Pheasant Phajitas

Dan Wood, Habitat Chairman, Central Indiana Pheasants Forever

Ingredients:
  1 pheasant
  1 pkg. fajita seasoning
  ½ cup olive oil
  1 15-oz. can Southwestern-style black beans
  ½ cup onion, chopped
  ¼ cup hot peppers (optional)
  1 package fajita shells
    Toppings such as shredded cheese, sour cream, tomatoes, shredded lettuce, olives and salsa

Step 1: Debone pheasant. Marinate in olive oil and half of fajita seasoning for several hours. Grill until done.

Step 2: Cut cooked pheasant into thin strips. In heavy iron skillet, mix pheasant strips, black beans, onion, remaining fajita mix and hot peppers. Heat on low and stir occasionally until warmed through. Serve in shells and top with desired toppings. Serves 4-5.

Game Day Pheasant

Jim Simpson, Tippe River Basin, Indiana,
PF Chapter 533

Ingredients:
   2 pheasants
   1 stick butter
5-6 cups half-and-half
2-3 Tbsp. flour
      Texas toast or mashed potatoes

Step 1: 30 minutes before the football game starts, heat oven to 325° F. Melt butter in roasting pan in oven. Break pheasant in half between breast and back legs. Stretch apart the back legs just enough to be able to lay flat in pan. Brown pheasant pieces in butter, turning to brown both sides.

Step 2: After the coin toss, pour 1 to 2 cups of half-and-half over pheasant. Cover. Bake for 45 minutes.

Step 3: During a commercial break, turn pheasant and sauce. Pour 1 to 2 cups half-and-half over pheasant. Bake 30 to 45 minutes more or until halftime.

Step 4: At halftime, pour 1 cup of half-and-half over pheasant, stir well. Make mashed potatoes. Bake pheasant another 30 to 45 minutes.

Step 5: During a commercial break, take pan out of oven and remove bones and tendons from pheasant. Pull apart meat and stir it well. If gravy is runny, mix 2 to 3 tablespoons of flour in ½ cup of half-and-half or milk and stir into pheasant. Continue baking until game is over. If the game goes into overtime, reduce heat to 225° F. and stir often. Serve over mashed potatoes or Texas toast.

Creamed Pheasant Sandwiches

Dave and Jan Hurley, Northeast Indiana Chapter 182

Ingredients:
   3 pheasant breasts
   ½ cup celery
      Salt
      Pepper
   1 14½-oz. can chicken broth
      Saltine crackers
      Honey buns

Step 1: Boil pheasant breasts in water with celery, salt and pepper. Cook until meat is ready to fall off the bone.

Step 2: Remove meat, cool, and shred into a separate pan. Add chicken broth and simmer for 20 minutes.

Step 3: In a resealable plastic bag, finely crush crackers. Add to pheasant mixture. (Use enough crackers to give the mixture a firm body.)

Step 4: Serve on honey buns with sliced onion and sweet pickles.

Wild Pheasant Stroganoff

William Garfoot, Pheasants Forever Chapter 148, Verona, Wisconsin

Ingredients:

- 2 small pheasants, cleaned, deboned, skinned and cut into bite-size pieces
- 4 cups milk
- 2 Tbsp. butter
- Salt and freshly ground black pepper to taste
- Onion powder to taste
- Garlic powder to taste
- 8 oz. fresh mushrooms, thickly sliced
- 1 10¾-oz. can condensed cream of mushroom soup
- ½ cup dry sherry
- 1 Tbsp. paprika
- ½ cup dry sherry
- ½ cup half and half
- 1 cup sour cream
- Buttered noodles

Step 1: Soak pheasant pieces in milk for 4 hours in refrigerator.

Step 2: Remove pheasant and pat dry; discard milk. In large skillet, melt butter and sauté pheasant pieces until lightly browned. Sprinkle with salt, pepper, onion powder and garlic powder.

Step 3: Add mushrooms and sauté for 2 minutes. Add soup and stir to coat. Pour in ½ cup sherry, making sure all pheasant pieces are covered with sauce. Sprinkle with paprika. Cover and simmer for 1 hour.

Step 4: Add remaining ½ cup sherry and stir well. With slotted spoon, remove pheasant to hot platter. Mix half and half and sour cream into sauce. Stir until well blended. Spoon over top of pheasant and serve immediately, accompanied by buttered noodles. Makes 4 servings.

Better Homes and Gardens® Test Kitchen

Grilled Quail Salad

Prep: 45 minutes   Marinate: 2 to 24 hours
Cook: 20 minutes   Grill: 12 minutes

Ingredients:
- 4 quail (about 1½ lb. total)
- ¼ cup extra-virgin olive oil
- 2 tsp. fresh sage, snipped
- ¼ tsp. salt
- ¼ tsp. freshly ground black pepper
- 2 oz. prosciutto, thinly sliced
- 4 red or purple plums, halved and pitted
- 8 oz. torn mixed baby greens (about 8 cups)
- 3 oz. Gorgonzola cheese, crumbled (¾ cup)
- ½ cup toasted walnuts
  Freshly ground black pepper

Step 1: Using kitchen shears, cut through backbone of each quail. Turn bone-side down and gently press down to flatten each quail. Arrange quail in a single layer in a shallow dish. For marinade, in bowl combine oil, sage, salt and pepper. Pour marinade over quail. Turn once to coat. Cover; marinate in refrigerator for 2 to 24 hours, turning quail occasionally. Prepare Port Dressing; set aside.

Step 2: Cut prosciutto lengthwise into 8 strips. Halve and pit 4 red or purple plums. Wrap prosciutto around plums, securing with toothpicks. Set aside.

Step 3: Drain quail; discard marinade. For charcoal grill, arrange medium-hot coals around drip pan. Place quail, bone side down, on rack above drip pan. Cover; grill 12 to 15 minutes or until no longer pink. Place plums over coals the last 4 minutes of grilling, turning once. (Or place quail on unheated rack of broiler pan. Broil 4 inches from heat 10 to 12 minutes or until no longer pink; turn once. Add plums last 4 minutes of broiling; turn once.)

Step 4: In a very large bowl toss half of the dressing with torn mixed baby greens. Divide among 4 plates. Top with quail halves and plums. Sprinkle with Gorgonzola cheese and toasted walnuts. Season with pepper. Serve with dressing.

Port Dressing: In a saucepan combine 1 cup port wine and 2 tablespoons finely chopped shallots. Simmer, uncovered, 20 to 25 minutes or until reduced to ¼ cup. Cool slightly. In a bowl whisk together port mixture, ½ cup extra-

virgin olive oil, 3 tablespoons red wine vinegar, 1 tablespoon balsamic vinegar, and ¼ teaspoon each salt and pepper. Makes 4 servings.

Nutrition Facts per serving: 998 cal., 71 g total fat (15 g sat. fat), 142 mg chol., 991 mg sodium, 36 g carbo., 5 g dietary fiber, 43 g protein.
Daily Values: 29% vit. A, 49% vit. C, 18% calcium, 48% iron.

*Cornish Game Hen Option: If quail are not readily available, substitute two 1¼- to 1½-pound Cornish game hens. Using kitchen shears, halve hens, splitting breast and backbone. Marinate hens for 6 to 24 hours. Grill hens as above about 50 minutes or until 180° F. (Or place hens, bone side up, on unheated rack of a broiler pan. Broil 5 to 6 inches from heat for 25 to 30 minutes or until 180° F. turning once.)

Grouse Burgundy

Bill Zehnder, Frankenmuth, Michigan

Ingredients:
- 1 cup burgundy or other dry red wine
- ½ cup soy sauce
- 2 cloves garlic, crushed
- 1 onion, sliced
- 1 tsp. Cajun seasoning
- ½ tsp. basil
- ½ tsp. oregano
- 5 grouse breasts, cut into 1-inch pieces
  Cooking oil
  Stir-fry vegetables such as carrots, cauliflower, green pepper, etc.

Step 1: Combine soy sauce, garlic, onion, Cajun seasoning, basil and oregano in resealable plastic bag. Add meat pieces. Seal and refrigerate overnight.

Step 2: Remove meat from bag and discard marinade. In a skillet or wok, stir-fry meat in oil until done. Set aside and keep warm. Stir-fry vegetables.

Step 3: Combine vegetables and meat. Serve with rice, cooked noodles or potatoes. Makes 10 to 12 servings.

Note: Stir-fry in small batches so the pan stays hot. Recipe can be used with sharp-tailed grouse or prairie chicken.

Southwestern Sharp-Tailed Grouse or Prairie Chicken

Leonard Zehnder, Charlevoix, Michigan

Ingredients:
- 1½ lbs. boned grouse or prairie chicken, cut into ½-inch to 1-inch cubes
- ¼ cup flour
- 1 Tbsp. paprika
- ¼ tsp. garlic salt
- 4 Tbsp. vegetable oil
- 1 large onion, cut into wedges
- 1 can beef broth
- 1 cup medium picante sauce
- ½ cup dry red wine
- ½ tsp. oregano

Step 1: Combine flour, paprika and garlic salt. Dredge meat in mixture and brown, a half at a time, in a skillet with 2 tablespoons oil. Place meat in a pot.

Step 2: Add onion to skillet and sauté. Sprinkle with additional flour mixture to thicken. Add to pot.

Step 3: Add broth, picante sauce, wine and oregano. Bring to a boil. Lower heat and simmer one hour in covered pot. Uncover pot for the last 10 minutes to thicken. Makes 6 servings.

Smoked Goose or Duck

Tim Tucker, Butler County Pheasants Forever Chapter 780, Hamilton, Ohio

Tucker says many people mistake this goose for roast beef. He says it's good with goose, better with duck, and great with sandhill crane.

Ingredients:

- 2 goose breast filets or 8 duck breast filets
- 1 can beer
- 2 tsp. salt
- 2 tsp. lemon juice
- 1 tsp. lemon-herb seasoning
- 1 tsp. meat tenderizer
- 1 tsp. crushed red pepper
- 1 tsp. ground mustard
- 1 tsp. vanilla flavoring
- 1 tsp. hot pepper sauce
- 1 tsp. soy sauce
- 1 tsp. Worcestershire sauce
- ½ tsp. maple flavoring
- 3 cups brown sugar
- 6 tsp. freshly ground pepper
- 1½ tsp. onion powder
- 1½ tsp. garlic powder

Step 1: In a large plastic or glass bowl (do not use metal bowl or pan), combine all ingredients except brown sugar, pepper, onion powder, and garlic powder. Add enough water to cover breasts. Marinate overnight in the refrigerator.

Step 2: Prepare charcoal smoker with a half pan of high-quality charcoal. Add hickory and mesquite chips that have been soaked in water for at least one hour to the charcoal. Coat the water pan inside and out along with the smoker grill with vegetable cooking spray for easier cleanup.

Step 3: Remove breasts from marinade and place on grill. Do not rinse. Save marinade.

Step 4: Combine brown sugar, pepper, onion powder and garlic powder. Sprinkle on top of breasts.

Step 5: Pour the remaining marinade in the water pan of the smoker. Smoke for 2 hours for goose or 1 hour for duck. Check occasionally for desired degree of doneness as this will vary with type of charcoal and outside temperature, but do not over cook.

Step 6: Let cool and slice in thin strips. Place on serving dish garnished with lemon slices and banana peppers. Serve with horseradish sauce (recipe follows) or a gourmet mustard sauce as an hors d'oeuvre.

Horseradish Sauce: Combine ½ cup mayonnaise, 3 tablespoons ground horseradish, ¼ teaspoon Tabasco sauce and the juice of ¼ lemon in a bowl and mix well. Garnish with fresh parsley or celery leaves and serve with smoked goose, venison or beef.

Better Homes and Gardens®

Test Kitchen

Rosemary Duck Breasts with Marinated Pears

Prep: 30 minutes   Chill: 12 to 24 hours
Grill: 23 minutes

Ingredients:
- 2 Tbsp. snipped fresh rosemary
- 1½ tsp. kosher salt
- ½ tsp. black pepper
- 2 cloves garlic, minced
- 4 boneless duck breasts with skin (about 1¾ lbs.)
- 2 large ripe pears
- 1 cup dry red wine
- ¼ cup sugar
- ¼ tsp. ground cloves
- ¼ tsp. ground ginger
- 1 cup oak wood chips
- 1 Tbsp. cracked green peppercorns (optional)

Step 1: For rub, in a small bowl stir together rosemary, salt, pepper and garlic. Sprinkle evenly over the meat side of each duck breast; rub in with your fingers. Cover and chill for 12 to 24 hours.

Step 2: Cut pears in half lengthwise, leaving stems intact. Remove core and peel pear halves. Place pear halves in a self-sealing plastic bag set in a shallow dish. For marinade, in a medium bowl combine wine, sugar, cloves and ginger. Pour over pears; seal bag. Marinate in refrigerator for 12 to 24 hours.

Step 3: At least 1 hour before grilling, soak wood chips in enough water to cover. Meanwhile, using a sharp knife, score skin sides of duck breasts diagonally to create a ½-inch-wide diamond pattern, making cuts about ¼-inch deep.

Step 4: Drain pears, discarding marinade. For a charcoal grill, arrange medium-hot coals around a drip pan. Test for medium heat above pan. Place pear halves, cut sides down, on grill rack over drip pan. Cover; grill for 8 to 10 minutes or until tender. (For a gas grill, preheat grill. Reduce heat to medium. Adjust for indirect cooking. Grill as above.) Remove pears from grill; set aside.

Step 5: Drain wood chips. Sprinkle wood chips over coals. Place duck breasts on grill rack over drip pan. Cover; grill for 15 to 18 minutes or until a meat thermometer registers 155° F. (For a gas grill, add wood chips according to manufacturer's directions. Grill as above.)

Step 6: Cut each pear half in half to form eight quarters. To make pear fans, use a sharp knife to make a series of ¹/₈-inch lengthwise slices in each pear quarter, starting from stem end and cutting to bottom (leave stem ends intact). Gently push down on each pear quarter to fan the slices.

Step 7: Serve duck on top of pears. If desired, garnish with green peppercorns. Makes 4 servings.

Nutrition Facts per serving: 787 cal., 68 g total fat (23 g sat. fat), 141 mg chol., 826 mg sodium, 17 g carbo., 3 g dietary fiber, 23 g protein.
Daily Values: 18% vit. A, 14% vit. C, 4% calcium, 26% iron.

Spring Gobbler Soup

Jim Hemm, Piqua, Ohio

Ingredients:

   Turkey leftovers
6 sage leaves
⅛ tsp. pepper
1 qt. chicken broth
5 stalks celery
3 large carrots
2 cups egg noodles
1 cup fresh asparagus
½ cup Morel mushrooms

Step 1: Cover all turkey leftovers — bones, juices and all — with water in a 4-quart pot. (Pheasant, quail or domestic turkey may also be used.) Unless the bird was roasted with sage, add sage leaves and pepper to the stock. Simmer the stock several hours until the meat falls off the bones. Strain the stock, cool and remove the fat. Separate the meat from everything else, dice into bite size, and return to the stock. Reduce the stock to a mild taste and add chicken broth.

Step 2: Dice celery and carrots and add to the stock. Add mushrooms and chopped asparagus. Simmer a half hour, then add egg noodles and simmer until the noodles are tender. Serves 4.

Skillet Turkey Sausage Dinner

Donald C. Squires, Kansasville, Wisconsin

Ingredients:

3-4 Tbsp. cooking oil
1¾ lbs. unpeeled red-skinned potatoes, cut into ½-inch cubes (about 5 cups)
2 medium onions, diced (1½ cups)
½ lb. fully cooked smoked turkey sausage, diagonally sliced ¼-inch thick
1 tsp. dried thyme
½ tsp. garlic powder
¼ tsp. salt
¼ tsp. pepper
¼-½ green bell pepper, diced
   Mushrooms, sliced, (optional)
   Seasoning salt, to taste
1 15-oz. jar of salsa (optional)

Step 1: Cover bottom of a 12-inch skillet with the oil. Cook potatoes and onions uncovered, over medium heat about 12 minutes or so, until potatoes are nearly tender, stirring occasionally.

Step 2: Add peppers, mushrooms and sausage, and additional oil as needed to prevent sticking. Cook uncovered about 10 minutes or until vegetables are tender and potatoes are slightly brown, stirring often. Stir in thyme, garlic powder, salt and pepper, and cook for 1 minute more. (Optional: Add a 15-ounce jar of salsa, heat through.) Serves 6.

Rabbit Barbecue

Neil W. Love, Frankenmuth, Michigan

Ingredients:
- 2-3 rabbits, cleaned and cut into pieces
  Cooking oil
- 2 large onions, chopped
- 3 Tbsp. Worcestershire sauce
- ½ tsp. dry mustard
- 2 Tbsp. brown sugar
- 2 15-oz. cans cooked tomatoes
- 2 Tbsp. cornstarch
- ½ tsp. salt
- ½ cup catsup
- ½ tsp. pepper
- ¼ cup vinegar

Step 1: Salt and pepper each piece of rabbit meat. Shake in a resealable bag with enough flour to coat. Brown in oil. Place in baking dish.

Step 2: In a separate pan, sauté chopped onions in additional oil until tender. Combine brown sugar and cornstarch and add to onions.

Step 3: Stirring constantly, gradually add ketchup, vinegar, Worchestershire sauce, dry mustard, tomatoes, salt and pepper to onion mixture.

Step 4: Cook slowly for 25 minutes on medium-low heat, or until slightly thickened, stirring often.

Step 5: Pour sauce over rabbit in baking dish. Cover and cook at 300° F. for 1½ hours, basting with sauce occasionally. Makes 5 to 6 servings.

Marinade for Venison

Paul Hagemann, Hurley, Wisconsin
My all-time favorite way of cooking venison is grilling the tenderloins or butt portions (all meat, no fat or connective tissue).

Ingredients:
- 1-2 pound venison loin or butt section
- ½ cup dry red wine
- ⅓ cup soy sauce
- ¼ cup olive oil
  Fresh ground black pepper to taste
- 2 garlic cloves, crushed (optional)

Step 1: Trim all fat, gristle, connective tissue, etc., from meat, then slice cross-grain into 1- to 2-inch medallions. Place meat in a shallow covered dish.

Step 2: Combine remaining ingredients. Pour over meat. Cover and refrigerate, turning meat every couple of hours. Allow meat to marinate overnight, or at least 4 hours.

Step 3: Grill to your liking. Discard marinade.

Venison Rouladen

Dorothy Zehnder, Frankenmuth Bavarian Inn, Frankenmuth, Michigan

Ingredients:

   8 oz. bacon, chopped
   8 oz. celery, chopped
   8 oz. onions, chopped
   1 tsp. Liquid Smoke
1-1½ lbs. round cut venison
  2½ oz. stone ground mustard
      Butter
      Dill pickle spears
      Cooking oil
   1 can beef broth
   3 Tbsp. cornstarch
   ¼ cup cold water or red wine

Step 1: For stuffing mixture, fry bacon in a large sauté pan over medium heat until bacon begins to brown. Add chopped celery and onions; cook until al dente. Remove from heat and add Liquid Smoke. Chill until cool enough to handle.

Step 2: Cut 8 to 10 thin slices of meat thin from the round cut. Use a meat mallet to pound each piece. (If round cuts aren't available, any thin medallion may be used.)

Step 3: Spread each medallion with mustard. Brush lightly with melted butter and top with 2 ounces of the stuffing mixture. Place a dill pickle spear into the middle of each and roll them up. Secure each roll with two toothpicks.

Step 4: Place a medium-size sauté pan over medium heat and add a generous amount of oil once the pan is hot. Carefully add the stuffed meat rolls. Brown on two sides, place into baking dish and set aside.

Step 5: Discard grease from pan. Add beef broth to pan and heat, scraping the remaining oil from the bottom of the pan. Pour the broth over the meat in the baking dish.

Step 6: Bake at 325° F. for 45 minutes to 1 hour or until the internal temperature reaches 160° F. Remove Rouladen from baking dish and keep warm.

Step 7: To make gravy, place liquid from baking dish into a small saucepan over medium heat. In a separate bowl, mix together cornstarch and water or wine. Gradually add to baking liquid while stirring constantly, until thickened and boiling. Pour warm gravy over Rouladen and serve.

Venison Roast

Mary Ann Simpson, Highland, Illinois

Ingredients:
- 1 venison roast
- 2 cans cream of mushroom soup
- 1 can water
- ½ cup barbecue sauce
- 1 Tbsp. Italian seasoning
- 1 Tbsp. parsley flakes
- 1 tsp. paprika

Step 1: Place venison roast in slow cooker.

Step 2: Combine remaining ingredients. Pour over roast. Cook on low for 8 to 10 hours, until very tender and falling apart. Sauce makes an excellent gravy.

Cubed Venison Steak

Ronald L. Long, President and Banquet Chairman, Pheasants Forever Northeast Indiana Chapter 182

Ingredients:
- Cubed venison steaks
- Onion salt
- ¼ cup soy sauce
- 3 Tbsp. honey
- 2 Tbsp. vinegar
- 1½ tsp. garlic salt
- ¾ cup vegetable oil

Step 1: Sprinkle meat with onion salt.

Step 2: Combine remaining ingredients. Place meat in liquid mixture, cover and refrigerate overnight. (For better results, vacuum seal in rectangular marinating canister.)

Step 3: Remove meat from marinade and cook on grill on the top grate. Do not overcook. Discard marinade.

Venison Stew Paprika

Cheryl Riley, PF Vice President of Education and Outreach, Hudson, Wisconsin

Ingredients

1½-3 lbs. venison stew meat, cut into 1-inch cubes (can also use beef)
½ cup flour
3 Tbsp. paprika
Salt and pepper to taste
2 Tbsp. butter
2 medium onions, chopped
2 cloves garlic
1 tsp. marjoram
1 11-oz. can tomatoes or 1 can tomato sauce
½ cup sour cream at room temperature
½ cup red wine
Egg noodles

Step 1: Shake meat cubes in plastic bag with flour, 1 tablespoon of the paprika, salt and pepper. In Dutch oven, melt butter and sauté coated venison cubes until browned. (You may have to brown the cubes in stages; avoid crowding them so they get nicely browned.)

Step 2: Remove cubes to warm dish and in the same Dutch oven, sauté onions with garlic and 2 tablespoons of the paprika until soft. Add marjoram, tomatoes and wine. Add browned venison cubes and simmer over low heat until meat is tender (45 minutes to 1½ hours).

Step 3: Just before serving, stir in ½ cup sour cream. Serve with egg noodles.

Note: Cheryl has taught Dutch oven cooking, and says all you need to prepare this recipe is a 12-inch Dutch oven (with feet), an aluminum pan (oil pans work well) and some charcoal briquettes. Get your charcoal white hot and then place about 12 briquettes in the aluminum pan in a circle and place Dutch oven on top. Add more hot briquettes if needed to sauté meat and onions. When ready to simmer, use about 8 briquettes on the bottom, place lid on oven and put 12 briquettes on top. When meat is tender and cooked through, add sour cream and serve over egg noodles. Remember to wash and dry your oven and store with lid ajar (or place briquette inside to absorb moisture).

Swiss Elk Steak

William Garfoot, Pheasants Forever Chapter 148, Verona, Wisconsin

Ingredients:
- 2 lbs. elk steak
- Flour
- 2 Tbsp. butter
- 1 15-oz. can tomato sauce
- ½ cup red wine or beef broth
- 2 Tbsp. Worcestershire sauce
- ½ cup onions, diced
- ½ cup green pepper, diced
- 1 2¼-ounce can sliced ripe olives, drained
- 1 cup sliced fresh mushrooms
- ½ tsp. salt
- ½ tsp. pepper
- 4 Swiss cheese, sliced (optional)
- Cooked noodles

Step 1: Dredge elk steak lightly in flour; shake off excess. Melt butter in large skillet; brown steak on both sides. Place in shallow baking pan.

Step 2: Combine the next 9 ingredients and pour over steak. Bake at 350° F. for 1½ to 2 hours or until desired tenderness. If desired, add Swiss cheese before serving. Makes 4 servings.

Note: This also can be made in slow cooker. Brown meat as above and place remaining ingredients (except cheese) in slow cooker.

The Northeast

Hunters have been bagging game in this part of the country since before the states were even colonies. With their Yankee ingenuity and a true love of the land, Northeasterners know hunting. They also appreciate a well-cooked meal, and have developed some delicious ways to prepare their banquet.

Pheasant Minestrone Soup

Jane Bryndel, Western Pennsylvania PF Chapter 630
You can use pheasant, grouse or even chicken if your shooting was bad. I only use the white meat of the bird for recipes and cook the leg meat for my dog, Abbey. She deserves it.

Ingredients:

- 1 pheasant, cooked and cut into bite-size pieces
- 2 14-oz. cans chicken broth
- 1 15-oz. can garbanzo or kidney beans
- 1 cup frozen vegetables
- 1 medium onion, chopped
- ½ cup small noodles
- 1 tsp. basil
- 1 tsp. garlic, chopped
- ¼ tsp pepper
- 1 14-oz. can Italian-style stewed tomatoes

Step 1: In a soup pot, stir together the broth, beans, vegetables, onion, pasta, basil and pepper. Bring to a boil, reduce heat and simmer for 10 minutes.

Step 2: Stir in the undrained tomatoes and the meat. Bring to a boil again, reduce the heat and simmer until the meat is done, probably about 10 minutes. Makes 4 servings. Serve with bread.

Who Would Prevail?

Keith Sanford, Wildlife Conservation Officer/Land Management Group Supervisor, Pennsylvania Game Commission

This past winter, Food and Cover Corps employees Jim Roberts, Marc Sechrist and I had the opportunity to travel to Montana to pick up some wild ringnecks for a trap and transfer pheasant restoration project in Northumberland, Montour and Columbia counties here in Pennsylvania.

On the trip home, we observed numerous species of wildlife including mule, deer, pronghorn antelope, prairie dogs, sharptailed grouse and magpies.

The most intriguing sight, however, was the mature bald eagle and adult Canada goose that we spotted together in a North Dakota cornfield. Both birds appeared to be equal in size. If time permitted, it would have been interesting to see how this encounter ended. Would goose have prevailed over eagle?

Pheasant a la Toaldo

Richard Toaldo, Central Jersey PF Chapter, Seaside Park, New Jersey.
This recipe was handed down from Richard's grandmother in Venice, Italy, in the early 1900s, to his father, Gino, and now to him. "I have continued the cooking of this recipe since my dad passed away in 1997 at 85 years of age," Richard says. "He and I hunted together from the time I was 12 years old, until two weeks before he died."

Ingredients:

- 1 pheasant
- 1 tsp. salt
- 1 tsp. pepper
- 1 onion
- ¼ cup raisins (white or red)
- 1 cup chicken broth
- 2 Tbsp. oil
  Pinch of sage
- ¼ cup pignoli nuts (pine nuts)
- ½ cup sherry or marsala wine

Step 1: Cut pheasant into eight pieces. Put oil and meat into a heavy covered frying pan (stainless steel or iron). Add salt, pepper, sage, pignoli nuts, raisins and sliced onion to meat. With one-half flame, brown meat on both sides. The pan should become a little tacky.

Step 2: When meat is browned, add wine and raise flame almost to highest point for about 1½ to 2 minutes. Using a metal spatula, scrape bottom of pan to keep from sticking.

Step 3: After loosening residue in bottom of pan, pour in chicken broth and let it come to a boil. Cover and let simmer for 30 minutes at reduced flame. Makes 4 servings.

Duck with Red Cabbage

Prep: 30 minutes   Cook: 1½ hours + 10 minutes

Ingredients:

- 3 lb. meaty domestic duck pieces (breast, thighs, and legs)
- 1 Tbsp. olive oil
- 4 bacon slices, cut up
- 1 large onion, thinly sliced
- 2 medium carrots, peeled and cut into chunks
- 1 clove garlic, minced
- 1 14-oz. can beef broth
- ½ cup dry red wine or beef broth
- 1 Tbsp. grape jelly
- 1 tsp. sugar
- ½ of a small head red cabbage
- 2 Granny Smith apples, cored and sliced

Step 1: Season duck pieces generously with salt and ground black pepper. In a Dutch oven brown duck pieces on all sides in hot oil. Drain off fat. Remove duck; set aside.

Step 2: Add bacon to Dutch oven; cook over medium heat until crisp. Drain off fat. Add onion, carrots, garlic, broth, wine, jelly and sugar. Bring to boiling.

Cut cabbage into 4 wedges. Add cabbage and duck to pan. Reduce heat to low. Simmer, covered, 1¼ hours. Add apples. Return to boiling; reduce heat. Simmer, covered, for 15 minutes or until duck is tender.

Step 3: Transfer duck to serving platter. Strain cabbage mixture, reserving juices. Spoon cabbage mixture onto platter with duck. Cover; keep warm. In Dutch oven bring juices to boiling; reduce heat. Simmer until desired consistency. Pour over duck and cabbage. Makes 6 servings.

Nutrition Facts per serving: 612 cal., 44 g total fat (15 g sat. fat), 129 mg chol., 669 mg sodium, 19 g carbo., 4 g dietary fiber, 32 g protein.
Daily Values: 53% vit. A, 41% vit. C, 7% calcium, 28% iron.

> There is a passion for hunting something deeply implanted in the human breast.

Charles Dickens

> # If some animals are good at hunting and others are suitable for hunting, then the Gods must clearly smile on hunting.
>
> **William Shakespeare**

Salad of Duck Confit with Pear Chutney and Warm Bacon Vinaigrette

Prep: 40 minutes   Bake: 20 minutes   Oven: 350°F.

Ingredients:

- 6 oz. boneless duck leg confit, 1-pound smoked turkey leg, or 1½-pound turkey thigh
- 8 cups torn frisée or mixed greens
- ½ cup pistachios, coarsely chopped
- 6 bacon slices, cut up
- 3 shallots, minced
- ¼ cup white wine vinegar
- 2 Tbsp. honey
  Pear Chutney (recipe follows)

Step 1: Place duck leg confit or smoked turkey leg in a 8×8×2-inch baking ban. Bake in a 350° F. oven for 20 to 25 minutes or until heated through and skin is crispy. (Or, place turkey thigh on rack in shallow baking pan; roast in 325° F. oven for about 1½ hours or until instant-read thermometer inserted in thickest portion and not touching bone registers 180° F.) Cut meat from bone and slice, discarding bone; keep warm.

Step 2: Meanwhile, in a large heatproof bowl, combine the torn frisée and pistachios. Set aside.

Step 3: For vinaigrette: In a large skillet, cook bacon over medium heat until crisp. Using a slotted spoon, remove bacon, reserving drippings in skillet. Drain bacon on paper towels; set aside. Add shallots to the reserved drippings in the skillet. Cook and stir over medium heat till tender. Stir vinegar and honey into drippings. Bring to boiling; remove from heat. Drizzle half of the vinaigrette over frisée and pistachios; toss to evenly coat.

Step 4: To serve, arrange frisée mixture on 4 large salad plates or 4 dinner plates. Top with bacon pieces. Arrange duck or turkey slices on top. Top each with about 2 tablespoons of the Pear Chutney. Drizzle with the remaining vinaigrette. Serve immediately. Makes 4 side-dish servings.

Nutrition Facts per serving: 444 cal., 28 g total fat (8 g sat. fat), 68 mg chol., 283 mg sodium, 31 g carbo., 4 g dietary fiber, 20 g protein.
Daily Values: 16% vit. A, 15% vit. C, 6% calcium, 15% iron.

Pear Chutney: In a large saucepan, combine 3 cups chopped and cored pears, 1 cup cider vinegar, 1 cup chopped red onion, ½ cup sugar, 1 tablespoon minced fresh ginger, 1 teaspoon ground coriander and ¼ teaspoon crushed red pepper. Bring to boiling; reduce heat. Simmer, uncovered, for 30 minutes or until liquid is nearly evaporated, stirring occasionally. Season to taste with kosher or sea salt and freshly ground black pepper. Serve immediately or cover and store in refrigerator for up to 1 week. Bring to room temperature before serving. Serve leftover chutney with pork or poultry. Makes about 2 cups.

Better Homes and Gardens®

Test Kitchen

> Go fish and hunt far and wide day by day—farther and wider—and rest thee by many brooks and hearth-sides without misgiving.

Henry David Thoreau

Maple-Glazed Quail

Prep: 10 minutes Marinate: 2 to 24 hours Grill: 15 minutes

Ingredients:

- 2 tsp. hot chili powder
- 1 tsp. dried thyme, crushed
- ¾ tsp. salt
- 8 quail, partially boned
- ½ cup pure maple syrup
- 2 Tbsp. peanut oil or cooking oil
-   Fresh pineapple wedges (optional)
-   Mixed fresh greens (optional)

Step 1: Combine chili powder, thyme and salt in a small bowl. Rub mixture into the quail. Place quail in a shallow baking dish. Combine half of the maple syrup and the oil; spoon over quail, turning to coat. Cover and chill for 2 to 24 hours.

Step 2: Prepare grill for indirect grilling; test for medium heat above the pan. Place quail, breast side down, on a lightly oiled rack over the drip pan. Cover and grill for 15 to 20 minutes or until an instant-read thermometer inserted into a quail reads 180° F. and juices run clear, turning and brushing once with remaining maple syrup.

Step 3: Serve with fresh pineapple wedges and mixed fresh salad greens, if desired. Makes 8 servings.

Nutrition Facts per serving: 299 cal., 17 g total fat (4 g sat. fat), 86 mg chol., 275 mg sodium, 14 g carbo., 0 g dietary fiber, 22 g protein.
Daily Values: 9% vit. A, 10% vit. C, 3% calcium, 25% iron.

Quail in Grape Leaves

Prep: 40 minutes   Grill: 25 minutes   Soak: 2 hours

Ingredients:

- ½ of a 16-oz. jar (16 leaves) brine-packed grape leaves
- ¼ cup olive oil
- 2 Tbsp. bottled minced garlic
- 4 tsp. dried herbes de provence, crushed
- 1 Tbsp. coarsely cracked black pepper
- 1 tsp. sea salt or ¾ teaspoon salt
- 8 4- to 4½-oz. semi-boneless quail
- 4 thin slices prosciutto, halved

Step 1: Gently rinse grape leaves in cold water. Place leaves in a medium bowl; add fresh cold water to cover. Soak for 1 hour; drain. Add fresh cold water to cover. Soak for 1 hour more. Gently rinse grape leaves; pat dry.

Step 2: In a small bowl combine oil, garlic, herbes de provence, pepper and salt. Brush half of the oil mixture over quail. Place 1 slice of prosciutto over the breast of each quail. Brush the prosciutto with some of the remaining oil mixture. Place 2 grape leaves on top of the prosciutto on each quail,

with the stem ends of the grape leaves at the tail end of each quail. Wrap leaves around each quail. Tie each quail lengthwise and crosswise with 100% cotton string. Brush each quail with the remaining oil mixture.

Step 3: For a charcoal grill, arrange medium-hot coals around a drip pan. Test for medium heat above pan. Place quail, breast side down, on grill rack over drip pan. Cover; grill for 25 to 30 minutes or until a meat thermometer inserted into the breast portion registers 170° F. (For a gas grill, preheat grill. Reduce heat to medium. Adjust for indirect cooking. Grill as above.)

Step 4: To serve, remove strings and discard grape leaves. Makes 8 servings.

Nutrition Facts per serving: 270 cal., 19 g total fat (4 g sat. fat), 81 mg chol., 388 mg sodium, 2 g carbo., 0 g dietary fiber, 22 g protein.
Daily Values: 5% vit. A, 11% vit. C, 3% calcium, 23% iron.

Better Homes and Gardens®

Test Kitchen

Maple-Cranberry Game Hens

Prep: 30 minutes   Marinate: 4 hours
Grill: 50 minutes   Stand: 10 minutes
Brining is a must-have technique for your grilling bag of tricks. Try it out with tender, juicy game hens and you can't go wrong.

Ingredients:
- 2 1¼- to 1½-lb. Cornish game hens
- 6 cups white cranberry juice or white grape juice
- ½ cup maple-flavored syrup
- ¼ cup coarse salt
-     string

Step 1: Remove giblets from game hens, if present. Rinse hens. For brine, in a stainless-steel or enamel stock pot or plastic container combine cranberry juice, syrup and salt; stir to dissolve salt.

Step 2: Carefully add game hens to brine. Cover and marinate in the refrigerator for 4 hours, turning hens occasionally.

Step 3: Remove game hens from brine; discard brine. Rinse hens and pat dry with paper towels. Tie drumsticks to tail with 100%-cotton kitchen string. Twist wing tips under back.

Step 4: For a charcoal grill, arrange medium-hot coals around a drip pan. Test for medium heat above pan. Place game hens, breast sides up, on grill rack over drip pan. Cover and grill for 50 to 60 minutes or until hens are no longer pink (180° F. in thigh muscle). (For a gas grill, preheat grill. Reduce heat to medium. Adjust for indirect cooking. Grill as above.)

Step 5: Remove game hens from grill. Cover with foil and let stand for 10 minutes before carving. Makes 2 servings.

Nutrition Facts per serving: 807 cal., 45 g total fat (12 g sat. fat), 346 mg chol., 1,180 mg sodium, 36 g carbo., 0 g dietary fiber, 59 g protein.
Daily Values: 6% vit. A, 100% vit. C, 4% calcium, 14% iron.

Better Homes and Gardens® Test Kitchen

Peppered Venison with Balsamic Prune Sauce

Prep: 10 minutes   Cook: about 10 minutes

Ingredients:
- 1 to 1½-lb. boneless venison loin chops or beef top loin steaks, cut ¾-inch thick
- 2 Tbsp. coarse grain mustard
- 2 tsp. mixed peppercorns, crushed
- 1 Tbsp. olive oil
- ¼ cup beef broth
- ¼ cup balsamic vinegar
- 3 Tbsp. brown sugar
- ¼ cup prunes, snipped
- 3 Tbsp. butter, cut up

Step 1: Cut meat into 4 serving-size pieces. Spread both sides of meat with the mustard; sprinkle with peppercorns.

Step 2: In a large skillet, heat oil over medium-high heat. Cook meat 3 to 4 minutes per side or until desired doneness. Remove from skillet; keep meat warm.

Step 3: Carefully add broth and vinegar to skillet, stirring to scrape up browned bits. Add sugar and prunes. Boil gently 3 to 5 minutes or until liquid is reduced by half. Whisk in butter to melt. Pour sauce over meat. Makes 4 servings.

Nutrition Facts per serving: 315 cal., 16 g total fat (7 g sat. fat), 121 mg chol., 299 mg sodium, 16 g carbo., 1 g dietary fiber, 27 g protein.

Better Homes and Gardens®

Test Kitchen

Pheasant, Rabbit and Squirrel Pot Pie

Melody Smith, President, Carroll County, Maryland, PF Chapter 622

Ingredients:

Pheasant, squirrel and rabbit meat, as is available, cooked and cubed
4   cups chicken broth
4   cups water (more or less as needed)
1   tsp. dried onions
1   tsp. salt
1   tsp. pepper
1   tsp. poultry seasoning
1   tsp. chicken seasoning salt
½   tsp. celery seed
1   cup carrots, chopped
1   cup potatoes, cubed
½   cup peas
    Flour
    Pie crusts, homemade or store-bought

Step 1: Add meat into pan of stock and water, add seasonings and cook for 10 minutes.

Step 2: Add remaining ingredients and cook for about ½ hour or until vegetables are tender.

Step 3: In separate bowl, mix flour and water and add to pot to thicken.

Step 4: Spread pie crust in large casserole dish, add stew, then top with remaining crust. Push edges together. Bake at 350° F. until crust is slightly brown, approximately 1 hour.

On the side
Crab-Stuffed Potatoes
Melody Smith, president, Carroll County, Maryland, PF Chapter 622

Ingredients:
- 12 large baking potatoes
- 1 lb. crab meat
- 1 cup butter or margarine, melted
- ½ cup mayonnaise
- 1 cup skim milk
- ½ cup sour cream
- 1 tsp. salt
- ¼ cup lemon juice
- ½ tsp. pepper
- ⅛ tsp. ground red pepper
- 2 bunches green onions
- ½ lb. bacon

Step 1: Preheat oven to 350°F. Prick potatoes, bake 1½ hours or until tender (or microwave).

Step 2: Cut potatoes in half lengthwise and scoop out centers, leaving ¼-inch shell.

Step 3: Beat centers in large mixing bowl until mashed. Beat in butter, milk, salt and pepper. Slice white part of onion, reserving green tops. Stir into potatoes. Spoon into shells and place on jelly-roll pan.

Step 4: Combine crab meat, mayonnaise, sour cream, lemon juice and red pepper in a large bowl. Mound crab meat mixture on stuffed potatoes. Press bacon pieces on top and bake for 40 to 45 minutes. Chop onion tops and sprinkle over potatoes. Serves 24.

The South

Hound dogs and hunting are engrained in the culture of the South. So is cooking. That perfect combination means that when somebody brings home a pheasant, deer or other prize from the field, a delicious dinner is just right around the corner.

Pheasant Breast Supreme

Start to Finish: 55 minutes

Ingredients:

- 4 medium skinless, boneless pheasant or chicken breast halves (1 lb. total)
- ¼ cup all-purpose flour
- ⅛ tsp. salt
- ⅛ tsp. pepper
- 3 Tbsp. butter
- ½ cup fresh mushrooms, sliced
- ¼ cup shallots, finely chopped
- ¼ cup celery, finely chopped
- ¼ cup cream sherry or chicken broth
- 2 tsp. lemon peel, finely shredded
- 3 Tbsp. lemon juice
- ½ cup chicken broth
- 1 cup whipping cream
- ¼ cup dairy sour cream
- 2 Tbsp. butter
- 2 cloves garlic, minced
- 6 cups fresh spinach, torn
- ¼ cup toasted almonds, sliced

Better Homes and Gardens®

Test Kitchen

Step 1: Place a pheasant or chicken breast, boned side up, between 2 pieces of plastic wrap. Working from the center to edges, very gently pound with the flat side of a meat mallet till ⅛-inch thick. Remove plastic wrap. Repeat with remaining pheasant or chicken.

Step 2: In a shallow dish, stir together flour, salt and pepper. Lightly coat pheasant or chicken on both sides with flour mixture; shake off excess.

Step 3: In a large skillet, melt 2 tablespoons of the butter. Cook pheasant or chicken, half at a time, over medium heat for 3 to 4 minutes until no longer pink, turning occasionally. Remove from skillet and keep warm.

Step 4: In the same skillet, add the remaining 1 tablespoon butter. Cook mushrooms, shallots and celery in hot butter for 5 to 6 minutes or till tender, stirring often. Carefully add the cream sherry or chicken broth, lemon peel and juice. Using a wooden spoon, stir and scrape up browned bits in skillet.

Step 5: Add the ½ cup chicken broth. Bring to boiling; reduce heat. Cook, uncovered, over medium-high heat for 6 to 8 minutes or until most of the liquid has evaporated (measures about 2 tablespoons), stirring often. Whisk in the whipping cream and sour cream. Cook, whisking constantly, over medium heat for 5 minutes or until mixture thickens and is reduced to about 1 cup. Return pheasant or chicken pieces to skillet; heat through.

Step 6: In a 12-inch skillet melt the 2 tablespoons butter. Add garlic; cook for 1 minute. Add the spinach. Using two spoons or tongs, toss 30 seconds or till spinach is coated and just wilted.

Step 7: To serve, evenly divide spinach among 4 warmed dinner plates. Place a pheasant or chicken piece on each bed of spinach; pour sauce over it. Sprinkle with almonds. Makes 4 servings.

Nutrition Facts per serving: 639 cal., 48 g total fat (g sat. fat), 194 mg chol., 455 mg sodium, 15 g carbo., 6 g dietary fiber, 35 g protein.

Charcoaled Pheasants

Jim Waters, Oklahoma

Ingredients:

- 2 pheasant breast fillets
- 1 can Sprite soda (not diet)
- ½ cup butter, melted
- ½ cup lemon juice
- 1 tsp. hot pepper sauce (optional)

Step 1: Combine all ingredients except pheasant in plastic or glass bowl or pan. Add pheasant. Cover and refrigerate for 2 to 6 hours.

Step 2: Stir pheasant and marinade. Heat until butter is melted and mixed with other ingredients.

Step 3: Place marinated pheasant breasts on medium to hot coals. Turn repeatedly and guard against burning. Remove when golden brown.

Pheasant and Wild Rice Casserole

Cinda Brent, Marianna, Arkansas

Ingredients:

- 2 pheasants, halved
- ½ cup garlic powder
  Milk
- 1 cup raw wild rice
- 1 can cream of chicken soup
- 1 can cream of mushroom soup
- 2½ cups water
  Water chestnuts, if desired
- 1 can mushrooms, if desired
- 1 pkg. instant onion soup mix, if desired

Step 1: Place pheasants in bowl, cover with milk and garlic powder. Refrigerate, tightly covered, for 24 to 30 hours. Discard milk.

Step 2: Mix rice, canned soups, water, mushrooms and water chestnuts in 9×13-inch glass casserole. Add pheasant. Sprinkle with onion soup mix. Cover lightly with foil. Bake 2 to 2½ hours at 300° F. Serves 6.

When you have shot one bird flying you have shot all birds flying. They are all different and they fly in different ways but the sensation is the same and the last one is as good as the first.

Ernest Hemingway

Frank's Grilled Quail Breast

Cinda Brent, Marianna, Arkansas

Ingredients:
- 12 quail breasts (may substitute dove breasts)
- 12 bacon slices, partially cooked but not crisp
- 6 mild to hot banana or jalapeño peppers, halved, without seeds
- Cream cheese or pepperjack filling for peppers
- Toothpicks

Step 1: Stuff pepper halves with cream cheese. Set aside.

Step 2: Wrap each quail breast and one pepper half tightly in one slice of partially cooked bacon. Secure with toothpicks as needed. Repeat assembly with remaining ingredients.

Step 3: Grill for 30 to 45 minutes over a low fire, turning once. If a grill is not available, they can also be baked in the oven at 350° F. for 30 to 45 minutes or until meat is fully cooked.

Tip: For best results with cheese, freeze the stuffed peppers before assembling them with quail breast and bacon. Cream cheese will hold up a little better than pepper jack. Makes 3 to 4 servings. Serve with barbecue sauce.

Grilled Quail Appetizer

Dale and Linda Garner, Quail Forever members, High Plains, Texas

Ingredients:
- Quail breasts
- Cheese, any kind
- Jalapeño pepper slices
- Bacon slices
- Dale's Seasoning Sauce
- Bottled Italian salad dressing

Step 1: Fillet meat off breastbone. Take a small piece of your favorite cheese and place on piece of breast meat along with a slice of jalapeño pepper.

Step 2: Roll up quail, cheese, and jalapeño. Wrap with bacon and secure with wooden toothpicks. Marinate in a 50/50 mixture of Dale's Seasoning Sauce and bottled Italian salad dressing for several hours or overnight.

Step 3: Grill over medium heat until ends of toothpicks begin to burn and bacon is cooked.

Grilled Caribbean Jerk Quail

Jim Scott, Tri-Cities Quail Forever Chapter 3030, Bristol, Tennessee

Ingredients:

    4 quail breasts (can substitute 2 pheasant breasts)
    4 bacon slices
    ½ cup yellow onion, roughly chopped
    1 jalapeño pepper, roughly chopped
    3 Tbsp. white wine vinegar
    2 Tbsp. soy sauce
    2 Tbsp. canola oil
    ½ tsp. ground allspice
    ¼ tsp. granulated garlic powder
    ¼ tsp. ground cinnamon
    ¼ tsp. kosher salt
    ¼ tsp. black pepper
    ⅛ tsp. ground nutmeg

Step 1: Combine all ingredients except quail and bacon in a food processor and blend until smooth. Makes about ¾ cup.

Step 2: Wrap quail breasts with bacon and secure with toothpick.

Step 3: Place breasts in glass or plastic dish (do not use metal) and cover with marinade. Refrigerate overnight.

Step 4: Grill over direct heat until meat is done.

Parmesan Quail

Luann Sewell Waters, Pheasants Forever and Quail Forever member, state Coordinator for Oklahoma Leopold Education Project

Ingredients:

    Breast meat from 5 quail, cut into bite-size pieces
    2 eggs
    ¾ cup cracker crumbs
    ¾ cup Parmesan cheese, grated
    1 tsp. black pepper
    1 tsp. garlic powder
    1 tsp. hot pepper sauce (optional)

Step 1: Beat eggs. Add hot pepper sauce, if desired.

Step 2: In separate bowl, mix all dry ingredients.

Step 3: Dip meat into egg, then roll in dry mixture. Place in lightly oiled Dutch oven. Bake for 30 to 40 minutes at 350° F.

When he was young, I told Dale Jr. that hunting and racing are a lot alike. Holding that steering wheel and holding that rifle both mean you better be responsible.

Dale Earnhardt

Crock Pot Quail in Wine-Herb Sauce

Cinda Brent, Marianna, Arkansas

Ingredients:
- 12 quail
- 3 Tbsp. flour
- Salt and pepper
- 1 large onion, sliced
- 2 slices lean smoked bacon, diced
- 1 clove garlic, crushed
- 1 4-oz. can sliced mushrooms, drained
- 1 bay leaf
- ½ tsp. leaf thyme
- ½ cup beef broth
- ½ cup dry white wine
- Chopped parsley

Step 1: Coat quail with a mixture of the flour, salt and pepper. Place onion slices in slow cooker; top with quail. Cover quail with diced bacon. Add remaining ingredients except parsley. Cover and cook on low setting for 6 to 8 hours.

Step 2: Remove quail to a heated platter and sprinkle with parsley. Thicken sauce, if desired, and spoon over quail. Makes 6 servings (about 3 quarts).

Quail Supreme

Cinda Brent, Marianna, Arkansas

Ingredients:
- ½ cup flour
- 1 tsp. salt
- ¼ tsp. pepper
- 6 quail, legs split from breasts
- ½ cup margarine, melted
- 1 medium onion, finely chopped
- ½ cup celery, finely chopped
- 4 cups cooked rice
- 1 Tbsp. poultry seasoning

Step 1: Combine flour, salt and pepper; pour into paper bag. Place several pieces of quail in bag; shake to coat.

Step 2: Brown quail in margarine; remove from pan. Sauté onion and celery in margarine. Add cooked rice and poultry seasoning; mix well.

Step 3: Form a bed for quail in rice; place quail on top. Cover; cook over low heat for 1 hour. Makes 6 servings.

Smothered Quail

Luann Sewell Waters, Pheasants Forever and Quail Forever member, State Coordinator for Oklahoma Leopold Education Project

Ingredients:

- 10 quail
- 2 bunches green onions, chopped
- 3 stalks of celery, chopped
- 7 mushrooms, sliced
- ½ cup butter
- 2 10½-oz. cans cream of celery soup
- 1 soup can of white wine
- Salt and pepper to taste

Step 1: Soak quail 3 to 4 hours in mild salt water.

Step 2: Sauté onions, celery, and mushrooms in butter for 10 minutes or until tender. Add cream of celery soup and wine and simmer for 10 minutes, stirring frequently. Add salt and pepper to mixture.

Step 3: Place drained quail in Dutch oven or large baking dish and pour sauce over them. Cover and cook for 1½ hours or until tender at 350° F. Serve birds over wild rice with sauce on top. Serves 6.

Talking Turkey from Texas to Taneytown

Melody Smith, President, Carroll County Maryland PF Chapter #622
Here is the story of one Northern woman's experience hunting in the South.
Thanks to Tammy Mowry, national coordinator for Women in the Outdoors, who invited me on the annual invitational three-day turkey hunt sponsored by the National Wild Turkey Federation, I was able to experience the Texan way of turkey hunting.

We were dropped off in the darkness outside El Dorado of the early morning chill, challenged to locate the feeders. Very little calling was necessary, since the birds were programmed to gather at the feeders at some point in the day or evening. We sat up against the largest of the bushes, all the while carefully avoiding the cactus and more importantly, any snakes. When the first golden rays peeked we expected the gobbling to begin but heard only one lone bird. The wind picked up, evaporating most of the sounds of Tammy's clucking and calling. A small family of bobwhite quail tentatively approached the feeder, quickly ate their fill and silently slipped away.

After lunch, the same procedure followed, the quail came and left as quietly as they had come. We couldn't say that for the cows, who successfully scared away our one lone gobbler who might have come to the feeder. Later as the darkness came Tammy's final call was echoed by a tom heading for his roosting place saying, "See you girls another day."

Days two and three were much the same — feeders but no birds. We just seemed to be in the wrong place at the wrong time. Tammy managed to nab a 23-pound tom during the final afternoon with Paul, a friend from Louisiana. We were delighted with her success as well as some of the other NWTF staff and their guests. They all had various turkey tales from Texas or from their home states. I could only sit and listen as some preferred using the old way of calling in the birds while others waited at the feeders.

I had missed opening day in Maryland, but in the early darkness of Thursday morning, my son, Steve, and I walked five minutes from home where I sat against that giant oak, toward an old logging path. A decoy bobbed quietly in the soft breeze as the gobbling began several ridges away. Soft clucks and purrs were soon heard coming from Steve's faithful box call as he enticed the tom to come closer. The forest sounds of song birds and woodpeckers were all that we heard until Steve began calling with his mouthpiece, emitting sounds only the gobbler finds endearing, then rustling feathers in the leaves and smacking them on his leg.

Out of nowhere, the bird appeared, silently walking on a carpet of white and pink star flowers with a backdrop out of a French Impressionist painting, the varying shades of budding greenery dotted by the lavender of the redbud trees and the contrasting white of the dogwood. The sun streamed through the tall oaks, spotlighting the glistening black of the bird giving me a prime shot at 32 yards away.

Steve jumped up excitedly yelling, "You got him, Mom, you got him!" At 7:00 a.m., April 17, 2007, I shot a 17-pound jake with two small beards. Now I have something to talk about.

Orange-Ginger Duck

Prep: 25 minutes   Marinate: 4 to 24 hours   Cook: 35 minutes   Roast: 15 minutes   Oven: 425° F.

Ingredients:

- 6 6- to 8-oz. duck breast halves
- 1 Tbsp. finely shredded orange peel
- 1 cup orange juice
- 1 cup dry white wine
- 6 Tbsp. honey
- 4 Tbsp. fresh ginger, grated
- 1 Tbsp. olive oil
- ¼ cup chicken broth
- 1 Tbsp. soy sauce
- 3 cups hot cooked rice

Step 1: Trim excess fat from duck (do not remove the skin); score skin. Place duck in a self-sealing plastic bag set in bowl. For marinade, combine orange peel, orange juice, ½ cup of the wine, 4 tablespoons of the honey and 3 tablespoons of the ginger. Pour over duck in bag; seal. Refrigerate 4 to 24 hours; turn bag occasionally.

Step 2: Remove duck from marinade; transfer marinade (about 1¾ cups) to a large saucepan. Add remaining wine. Bring to boiling; reduce heat. Boil gently, uncovered, 20 to 25 minutes or until reduced to 1¼ cups (watch carefully as mixture may foam over).

Step 3: Preheat oven to 425° F. In 12-inch skillet heat oil over medium-high heat; add duck. Cook about 10 minutes or until browned, turning once (watch for spattering). Transfer duck, skin side up, to a 9×13-inch baking pan. Roast for 15 minutes or until an instant-read thermometer registers 170° F. covering loosely with foil if duck begins to spatter.

Step 4: Meanwhile, for glaze, add remaining honey, remaining ginger, broth and soy sauce to reduced marinade. Return to boiling; boil gently, uncovered, about 15 minutes or until reduced to ²/3 cup; stir frequently. Season to taste. Slice duck breasts and place on rice; spoon glaze over duck.

Nutrition Facts per serving: 469 cal., 15 g total fat (4 g sat. fat), 154 mg chol., 402 mg sodium, 46 g carbo., 1 g dietary fiber, 31 g protein.
Daily Values: 3% vit. A, 45% vit. C, 3% calcium, 28% iron.

Better Homes and Gardens®

Test Kitchen

Spinach Salad with Duck Breast

Better Homes and Gardens®

Test Kitchen

Aromatic herbs and other flavors meld seamlessly in this delicious salad. For a different taste, try grilling the duck breast.

Ingredients:
- 2 6 to 8-oz. boneless duck breasts
   Salt and fresh ground pepper
- 4 cups torn fresh spinach
- 3 oz. chevre (goat cheese), crumbled
- ½ cup fresh chervil or parsley, chopped
- ¼ cup toasted pine nuts
- 3 Tbsp. fresh cilantro or basil, snipped
- 3 bacon slices
- ¼ cup red wine vinegar
- 1 tsp. sugar
- ½ tsp. salt
- 2 Tbsp. oil-packed dried tomatoes, drained and chopped

Step 1: Season duck breast with salt and pepper. Place duck in a 9×9×2-inch baking pan. Roast in a 375° F. oven for 50 minutes or until thermometer registers 180° F. Remove from pan.

Cool slightly. Remove any excess fat from meat; discard. Cut meat into bite-size pieces.

Step 2: Meanwhile, in a large salad bowl combine spinach, chevre, chervil, pine nuts and cilantro; set aside.

Step 3: For the dressing, in a large skillet cook bacon until crisp. Reserve 2 tablespoons of drippings in skillet. Crumble bacon; set aside. Stir vinegar, sugar and the ½ teaspoon salt into drippings. Bring to boiling; remove from heat. Pour over spinach mixture.

Step 4: Add duck and reserved bacon; toss gently to coat with dressing. Sprinkle with tomatoes. Makes 4 to 6 servings.

Duck and Asian Pear Salad with Pecan Goat Cheese

Prep: 35 minutes   Broil: 10 minutes
The honey-peach salad dressing gives this salad a delicious Southern flavor.

Ingredients:

- 4 6.5- to 7.5-oz. boneless domestic duckling breasts or 4 small skinless, boneless chicken breast halves
-    Honey-Peach Salad Dressing (recipe follows)
- ¼ cup finely chopped pecans, toasted
- 1 4-oz. log goat cheese
- 8 cups shredded Napa cabbage or shredded Romaine or leaf lettuce
- 1 medium Asian pear, tart apple or firm-ripe pear, cored and thinly sliced lengthwise
- 4 kiwi fruit and/or golden kiwi fruit, peeled and sliced lengthwise into wedges

Step 1: Remove skin and fat from duckling. Place duckling or chicken breast halves on the unheated rack of a broiler pan. Broil 4 to 5 minutes from the heat for 10 to 12 minutes or until an instant-read thermometer inserted in duck registers 155° F., turning once (broil chicken for 12 to 15 minutes or till thermometer registers 170° F., turning once). Cool about 15 minutes; cut duckling or chicken into thin, bite-size pieces. Set aside.

Step 2: Meanwhile, prepare Honey-Peach Salad Dressing. Roll cheese in pecans until coated. Slice cheese into 8 slices.

Step 3: To serve, divide salad greens among 4 dinner plates or bowls. Arrange duck or chicken, Asian pears, kiwi and cheese on top of the greens. Serve dressing with salads. Makes 4 main-dish servings.

Nutrition Facts per serving: 626 cal., 33 g total fat (8 g sat. fat), 216 mg chol., 370 mg sodium, 36 g carbo., 6 g dietary fiber, 48 g protein. Daily Values: 11% vit. A, 208% vit. C, 21% calcium, 45% iron.

Honey-Peach Salad Dressing: In a small food processor or blender, combine 3 tablespoons honey; 3 tablespoons peach nectar, pear nectar or peach liqueur; 1 tablespoon lemon juice; 1 clove garlic; ¼ teaspoon sea salt or salt; and ¼ teaspoon ground black pepper. Cover and process or blend till smooth. With processor or blender running, gradually add ⅓ cup olive oil and process or blend till combined. Serve immediately or cover and store in refrigerator for up to 1 week. Stir just before serving. Makes about ¾ cup.

Pan-Seared Duck Breast with Peppered Apples

Prep: 25 minutes   Bake: 10 minutes   Cook: 20 minutes
Oven: 350° F.

Ingredients:

- 4 Golden Delicious apples, peeled if desired, and sliced
- ¼ cup butter
  Ground black pepper
- 4 boneless duck breasts (with skin)
  Salt and ground black pepper
- ½ cup apple balsamic vinegar or balsamic vinegar
- 4 cups bitter greens

Step 1: In a very large oven-going skillet cook apples in hot butter over medium heat for 10 minutes or until golden brown and tender, stirring frequently. Season to taste with pepper; remove from skillet and set aside.

Step 2: Score the skin side of the duck breasts at ½-inch intervals in a diamond pattern. Season duck breasts with salt and pepper.

Step 3: In the same skillet, cook duck breasts, skin side down, over medium heat for minutes; turn. Cook 5 minutes more or until browned. Drain fat. Place pan in a 350° F. oven for 10 to 15 minutes or until an instant-read thermometer registers 140° F. Remove duck from pan; cover and let stand for 10 minutes (the meat's temperature will rise 5° F. during standing time). Add vinegar to drippings in skillet, scraping up browned bits. Return skillet to burner over medium-high heat. Bring to boiling and cook until liquid is reduced by half.

Step 4: Slice duck breasts. To serve, spread bitter greens on a serving platter. Top with peppered apples and duck breast slices. Drizzle sauce over all. Makes 4 servings.

There's just about nothing easier – or tastier – than a roast. Here are three different ways to prepare your favorite wild game roast, each with a unique Southern flavor.

Southern-Style Roast

Carter Stults, Nemaha Valley Nebraska PF Chapter President, Nebraska State Council Treasurer
Although this recipe was submitted by a Nebraskan, the taste is purely Southern!

Ingredients:
- 4- to 8-pound deer or elk neck roast
  Heavy Brine* (salt and water mixture)
- 1 bottle of your favorite Southern-style marinade, like Dale's Seasoning, Moore's Sauce, Johnny Fleeman's, or Bullard's Louisiana Supreme Marinade
  Spices to taste, such as Tony Chachere's Original Creole Seasoning, crushed red pepper, paprika or cayenne pepper
  Vegetables such as red potatoes, garlic, carrots, celery and onions

Step 1: Prepare roast by piercing with an ice pick or filet knife. Prepare a heavy brine by rapidly stirring cold water while adding salt until salt stops dissolving. Soak roast for 2 hours in heavy brine, then remove and rinse.

Step 2: Soak roast overnight in the marinade of choice. Remove roast and discard marinade. Preheat oven to 350° F.

Step 3: In a covered roasting pan, place rinsed vegetables in bottom of pan and cover with 1 inch of water. Sprinkle spices over top half of roast and place roast on top of vegetables. For a 6- to 8-pound roast, cook in oven for 1½ hours at 350° F. and 1 hour at 250° F. For a 4- to 6-pound roast, cook for 1¼ hour at 350° F. and 45 minutes at 250° F. For a true Southern meal, serve with cornbread and sweet tea.

Crock Pot Deer Roast

Luann Sewell Waters, Pheasants Forever and Quail Forever member, State Coordinator for Oklahoma Leopold Education Project

Ingredients:
- 1 can cream of mushroom soup
- 1 can Rotel tomatoes
- 1 pkg. dry onion soup mix
- 1 Tbsp. BV broth & sauce concentrate
- 3-4 lb. venison roast
- 2 small cans whole green chilies, cut in half lengthwise

Step 1: Mix first four ingredients together in slow cooker. Add roast and spoon mixture over it. Roast should be almost covered by mixture. Top with chilies. Bring to a boil.

Step 2: Turn heat to low and cook overnight. Serve with pasta or rice.

Deer Roast

Si Murphree, Birmingham, Alabama
"I am the chairperson for Ducks Unlimited in Birmingham and I am very proud of what you guys are doing with the conservation efforts," Murphree writes. "Our organizations will make remarkable differences in our world."

Ingredients:

Deer roast, preferably ham or shoulder
2 bottles Dale's or Moore's marinade
4 cups red wine
2 cans Coca-Cola
1 large bottle cayenne pepper
1 large bottle chili powder
1 large bottle garlic salt

Step 1: In a large pan, combine bottled marinade, wine and cola. Roll meat in marinade until completely covered.

Step 2: In a dry aluminum pan, combine spices and spread over bottom of pan. Roll roast in spice mix until every inch is covered.

Step 3: Place roast on a hot grill to sear all sides. It's okay to burn it a little.

Step 4: Wrap the meat in aluminum foil tightly to seal in the juices. Cook at 300° F. oven for 4 to 6 hours. Remove and allow to sit for one hour. Open foil carefully, as juices will still be hot. Meat is done when the bone comes out with no meat attached.

Note: If you do not have a deer roast available, a Boston butt will also work nicely.

Barbecue Bison Ribs with Sorghum-Bourbon Sauce

Here's a decidedly Southern twist on a Western favorite: Bison.
Prep: 20 minutes   Chill: 8 to 24 hours   Grill: 1¼ hours

Ingredients:
- 4-5 lbs. bison ribs
- 1 Tbsp. salt
- 1 Tbsp. black pepper
- 2 tsp. garlic powder
- 4-6 cups hickory wood chips
- 1 recipe Sorghum-Bourbon Sauce (below)

Step 1: Trim fat from ribs. For rub, in a small bowl combine salt, pepper, and garlic powder. Sprinkle rub evenly over both sides of ribs; rub in with your fingers. Cover and chill for 8 to 24 hours.

Step 2: At least 1 hour before grilling, soak wood chips in enough water to cover.

Step 3: Drain wood chips. For a charcoal grill, arrange medium-hot coals around a drip pan. Test for medium heat above pan. Sprinkle drained wood chips over coals. Place ribs, bone sides down, on grill rack over drip pan. (Or place ribs in a rib rack; place on grill rack.) Cover; grill for 1¼ to 1½ hours or until ribs are tender, brushing twice with ½ cup of the Sorghum-Bourbon Sauce during the last 30 minutes of grilling. (For a gas grill, preheat grill. Reduce heat to medium. Adjust for indirect cooking. Grill as above, except place ribs in a roasting pan.)

Step 4: To serve, reheat remaining Sorghum-Bourbon Sauce until bubbly; pass with ribs. Makes 4 to 5 servings.

Nutrition Facts per serving: 436 cal., 6 g total fat (2 g sat. fat), 141 mg chol., 2,935 mg sodium, 38 g carbo., 2 g dietary fiber, 53 g protein.
Daily Values: 17% vit. A, 24% vit. C, 5% calcium, 43% iron.

Sorghum-Bourbon Sauce: In a medium saucepan stir together ⅓ cup sorghum, ¼ cup strong coffee, ¼ cup bourbon, 2 tablespoons white wine Worcestershire sauce, 2 teaspoons dry mustard, 1 teaspoon onion powder, and ¼ teaspoon bottled hot pepper sauce. Bring to boiling, stirring frequently. Stir in 1½ cups catsup. Return to boiling; remove from heat.

Better Homes and Gardens®

Test Kitchen

The West

This is where the pheasant got its start in America. Since the initial release of Chinese ringnecks into Oregon's Willamette Valley in 1881, hunters have taken great pleasure in harvesting the beautiful birds. Some things never change.

Bourbon-Buffalo Pheasant Strips

Ed Boyle of Londonderry, New Hampshire, submitted this recipe for a snack served at the Flying B Ranch in Kamiah, Idaho.

"I spent a week at the Flying B Ranch in October of 2006 on the hunt of a lifetime," Ed says. "I hunted mule deer, fished for steelhead and spent a day bird hunting on the ranch for pheasant and partridge."

Ingredients:

- 4 pheasant breasts
- 1 cup flour
- 1 Tbsp. salt
- 1 tsp. pepper
- ½ yellow onion, diced
- 2 Tbsp. butter
- ¼ cup bourbon
- ⅓ cup brown sugar
- ⅔ cup Frank's Red Hot sauce

Step 1: Clean and check for shot in pheasant breasts. Cut each breast into 4 or 5 pieces. Dredge pieces in flour seasoned with salt and pepper. Fry in 360° F. oil until golden brown. Place on paper towel and sprinkle with a dash of salt.

Step 2: For bourbon sauce, sauté onion in butter over medium-high heat for a couple of minutes, stirring frequently. Add bourbon; mix well. Add brown sugar; cook on low heat until sugar has dissolved. Add hot sauce; simmer for 5 minutes on low heat.

Step 3: Toss the finished pheasant strips with bourbon sauce and serve with bleu cheese or ranch dressing and celery.

Pheasant Poppers

Bob Crandall, president of Pheasants Forever Chapter 57, Sidney, Montana

"Over the years, I have never seen a piece left in the serving dish, and I have fed this to maybe 200 hunters," Bob says.

Ingredients:

Ingredient quantities vary depending on how much pheasant is available.

Pheasant breasts, cut into 1-inch cubes
Egg
Bread crumbs or cornflake crumbs
Butter
Worcestershire sauce

Step 1: Drench pheasant breast cubes in beaten egg and roll in bread crumbs or cornflake crumbs. Repeat.

Step 2: Heat a 50/50 mixture of butter (not margarine) and Worcestershire sauce in a skillet.

Step 3: Fry breaded pheasant pieces in skillet, turning once, until golden brown. Serve immediately.

Pheasant Breast with Artichoke Sauce

Fred Tullis, Rodeo, New Mexico
Fred is a chef at Price Canyon Dude Ranch in Douglas, Arizona.

Ingredients:

- 4 pheasant breasts, boned
- ½ cup flour
- 2 tsp. each salt and pepper
- 2 tsp. garlic powder
- ½ stick butter
- Orange slices and tarragon sprigs for garnish

Step 1: Add salt, pepper and garlic powder to flour. Dredge pheasant breast in flour mixture. In a large frying pan, melt butter and sauté the breasts over medium-high heat until browned, approximately 3 minutes per side. Use the same frying pan with drippings to make the following sauce.

Artichoke Sauce Ingredients:

- ½ stick butter
- 1 cup onion, chopped
- 2 cloves garlic, minced
- ½ cup white wine
- 1 cup chicken broth
- ¼ cup heavy cream
- 1-2 Tbsp. roux
- 1 15-oz. can artichoke hearts, marinated in oil, drained
- 2 Tbsp. tarragon, chopped (add more if desired)
- Salt and pepper to taste

Step 2: Melt the butter, add onions and sauté for about 3 minutes on medium heat. Add garlic and cook for 2 more minutes, stirring occasionally. Add the wine; increase heat to high to cook off the alcohol. Add chicken broth and cook on high for another 3 minutes. Add the heavy cream and cook until the sauce thickens, about 1 minute, stirring constantly. Add the roux, a little at a time, for desired thickness. Adjust with chicken broth if necessary.

Step 3: Add artichoke hearts and pheasant breasts, and simmer for 2 minutes, or to heat through. Add tarragon, salt and pepper to finish. Place breasts on serving dish, garnish with orange slices and additional tarragon. Serve with rice and a vegetable. Serves 4.

A true conservationist is a man
who knows that the world
is not given by his fathers,
but borrowed from his children.

John James Audubon

Topless Pheasant Pot Pie

Craig Roberts, President of Central Montana PF Chapter 417 and wife Cathy, Lewistown, Montana,

Ingredients:
- 1 pheasant
- 2 medium onions
- 4 stalks celery
- Salt
- Pepper
- 1 Tbsp. + ½ stick butter
- 3 Tbsp. flour
- 1 tsp. Worcestershire sauce
- Yellow food coloring
- 1 can sliced mushrooms
- Pastry for single-crust pie

Step 1: Place pheasant, one onion, two stalks of celery, and salt and pepper to taste into a large pot. Cover with water and boil until pheasant is tender. Remove pheasant from broth, strip meat from bones and dice into large pieces. Strain and reserve three cups of broth.

Step 2: Finely dice the second onion and remaining celery. Sauté in 1 tablespoon butter until tender but not brown.

Step 3: Bring strained broth to a boil. In a separate pan, melt ½ stick of butter and add flour. Stir until well blended, without browning. While mixture is hot, add to boiling broth. Stir well until thick and smooth.

Step 4: Remove thickened broth from heat and add Worcestershire sauce and a few drops of yellow food coloring.

Step 5: Add sautéed onion and celery. Add mushrooms.

Step 6: Place diced pheasant in a pie pan or casserole dish. Pour thickened broth over meat and cover with pie crust. Bake at 450° F. until pie crust is brown. If desired, omit pie crust and serve casserole over rice.

Super Rooster

Walt Bodie, former PF regional biologist for Idaho, Nevada, Utah and Washington

There are many memorable roosters that stand out in my mind, but none so much as the one I never brought to bag.

I first met him, hereafter called SR (Super Rooster), on an island in the Snake River of southwest Idaho. I was hunting ducks over decoys on the upstream end of a 30-acre island. SR started cackling behind me just after dawn on that warm mid-November morning. I thought Sandy, her brother Mack, and I would get that noisy bird when the duck shooting slowed down.

If only I had known then what I later learned about SR, I would have packed up my decoys and moved to another island. Mental health would have demanded it. He would be there every time I visited the island and he was always noisy. He taunted us. It got to the point where Sandy would duck her head and crawl under the blind seat when he started cackling.

Mack didn't care. A bird was a bird to Mack. He was not the serious pheasant hunter that Sandy was. I hunted that bird by myself at first, but later called in reinforcements, first a single friend and finally a group of six friends with five dogs for a strategic assault on SR. We tried blocking all the likely exits from the island; SR went out the most unlikely exit and escaped to the mainland. He never used the same exit twice. We had over 30 days to bag that bird, but he beat us every time.

What we came to find out is that pheasants spend most of their time on the mainland and only move to the islands after the crops are harvested and heavy hunting pressure moves them to the safety of the willow and brush-choked islands. Only the smart ones survive that long. The following year when I pulled the boat onto the island on the opening morning of duck season, Sandy refused to get out of the boat. I thought about it for a moment, then pushed off to find another island to duck hunt. Live in peace, SR!

Honey Mustard Pheasant with Thyme

Joel Leidecker, professor at Santa Clara University, Santa Clara, California

Ingredients:
- 2 pheasant breast filets
- 1 cup buttermilk
- 2 Tbsp. oil
- 2 Tbsp. Dijon mustard
- 2 tsp. green peppercorns, crushed
- 4 tsp. honey
- ½ cup bread crumbs
- 4 tsp. + 1 Tbsp. butter
- Hot pepper sauce
- ½ cup white wine
- 1 Tbsp. ground thyme
- 1 cup chicken or pheasant stock

Step 1: Soak pheasant breast filets overnight in buttermilk in the refrigerator.

Step 2: Remove filets and pat dry with paper towels. Sear pheasant in a skillet with 2 tablespoons very hot oil, 10 seconds per side. Place breasts in a baking or casserole dish and bake at 350° F. for 10 minutes.

Step 3: Remove pheasant from the oven. Top breasts with mustard, peppercorns, honey, bread crumbs and butter. Add hot pepper sauce to taste. Return to 450° F. oven for a few minutes or until done.

Step 4: Heat wine and ground thyme on medium, reducing to about a tablespoon of liquid. Add stock and reduce on medium-high to a light syrup. Whisk in 1 tablespoon butter and 3 drops of hot pepper sauce. Drizzle over sliced breasts and serve.

Lemon-Rosemary Pheasant

Bill Vanderbilt, Ketchum, Idaho

Ingredients:
- 2 pheasant breasts and 2 thighs, boned
- 1½ cups olive oil
- 4 Tbsp. Dijon mustard
- ½ cup lemon juice
- 6 garlic cloves, minced
- ¼ cup chopped fresh rosemary or 2 Tbsp. dried rosemary
- 2 tsp. freshly ground black pepper

Step 1: In a small bowl, whisk oil and mustard together. Add remaining ingredients except for pheasant and mix well. (Can be stored in refrigerator for up to 2 weeks.)

Step 2: Marinate pheasant in mix for 3 hours at room temperature or overnight in the refrigerator.

Step 3: Remove meat from marinade and sauté in a small amount of oil over medium-high heat until tender. Slice and serve over a bed of risotto.

Plum Good Pheasant

Edward Junker, Bernalillo, New Mexico, PF and QF member.

I made this up one evening after my grandson turned up his nose at the suggestion of pheasant for dinner. It should work well with grouse or quail too.

Ingredients:

- 1 cleaned pheasant, with or without skin
- 3-4 Tbsp. butter
- 1 bottle Henry Weinhard's or other vanilla cream soda
- 8 fresh plums, peeled, skinned and pitted; or canned pitted
- ½ cup yellow onion, diced
- 2 Tbsp. butter
- Cooked linguini noodles
- ½-⅓ cup half and half
- Salt and pepper to taste
- 1 Tbsp. cornstarch

Step 1: Cut pheasant in half, or bone it out in big chunks. Cook on grill until meat is done, or cook in a large skillet with 3-4 tablespoons butter, turning often.

Step 2: Meanwhile, in a saucepan, place soda, plums, onion, and 2 tablespoons butter. Cook over low heat so it reduces to half as the bird cooks.

Step 3: When the pheasant is done, bone it out and cut into large chunks. Place meat into saucepan. Cook at a slow boil for about 10 minutes.

Step 4: Drain the sauce off the meat into another saucepan. Place the meat over linguini noodles.

Step 5: Add half-and-half, salt and pepper to sauce in pan. Stir constantly while heating it to a slow boil. As it begins to boil, add cornstarch that has been dissolved in ⅛ cup cool water. Stir constantly over steady medium heat until it thickens nicely. Pour sauce over the meat and noodles.

Sometimes the most memorable hunts are not those during which the most birds are harvested, but a one-bird day over a splendid point followed by an exceptional retrieve.

Craig E. Roberts, President, Central Montana PF Chapter 417

Pheasants and Fungi

Charlie and Donna Fitzgerald, Las Vegas, Nevada

Ingredients:

- 1 .5-oz pkg. dried forest mushroom blend (or 1-2 oz. sliced fresh mushrooms)
- 1 .5-oz. pkg. dried shiitake mushrooms (or 1 2-oz. sliced fresh mushrooms)
- 2 Tbsp. extra virgin olive oil
- 1 pheasant – boned out, skinned and cut into small chunks (¾ inch-1inch)
- 1½ tsp. minced garlic (fresh is best)
- 1 tsp. dried basil (or 1 oz. chopped fresh)
- 2 Tbsp. butter
- ¼ cup shallots, finely minced
- 1 Portobello mushroom cap, chopped into 1-inch pieces
- 3 Tbsp. oil-packed sun-dried tomatoes, sliced
- 2 Tbsp. arrowroot powder
- Salt and coarse pepper to taste

Step 1: In a small bowl, reconstitute dried mushrooms in water according to package instructions. Drain and reserve the water. Chop reconstituted mushrooms into small pieces. If using fresh mushrooms, quick wash and pat dry on paper towels.

Step 2: Heat olive oil in a large heavy skillet over medium heat. Sauté pheasant meat with garlic and basil until lightly browned. Remove meat from pan with a slotted spoon, and set aside.

Step 3: Add butter to oil in skillet. Sauté shallots, mushrooms and Portobello mushroom until golden brown. Stir in sun-dried tomatoes, and all but ¼ cup of the mushroom soaking water. Dissolve arrowroot powder in water, and stir into mushroom mixture.

Step 4: Return pheasant meat to skillet, and simmer 30 minutes. Serve with a California Merlot.

Ginger Pheasant
Tonya Linares, Salinas, California

Ingredients:
- 4 small chunks crystallized ginger
- ¾ cup soy sauce
- 3 medium-size cloves of garlic
- 2 cups water
- ¼ cup rice vinegar
- 1 pheasant cut up in pieces (legs, thighs, breasts, wings, etc.)
- Short grain white rice, steamed

Step 1: Slice crystallized ginger in thin pieces, crush gloves of garlic and add all ingredients to a medium-size stock pot. Simmer on low for 1 hour. Add water if it boils down to keep a sauce while cooking.

Step 2: Dish the white rice onto plate and dish out a couple of pieces of pheasant and spoon some of the sauce it was cooked in over the meat and rice.

A Woman's First Hunt
Tonya Linares, Salinas, California

After losing my father to cancer, I decided to go hunting for the first time, with a group of women. I found a Women on Target pheasant hunt on the NRA Web site to be held at Turk Station in Coalinga, California. My husband supported my going on a women's hunt to reacquaint myself with shooting, as my dad had taught me in childhood.

I drove 90 minutes from my home on my own on a Friday morning, and when I arrived at the beautiful Turk Station Lodge, I was pleased to find the greatest amenities: a cook, guides and great scenery. A perfect way to start a wonderful experience in hunting. It was apparent that the other ladies were also new at this, so I was not alone. We were served a spectacular dinner and rested up for our before-dawn hunting trip.

We all became friends and helped each other out and had a great morning, as each of us were successful bringing in birds. We enjoyed seeing the sunrise and the beautiful outdoors and the long walks through the fields, seeing other wildlife, and forming forever friendship bonds with strangers turned friends. We went back to the lodge for yet another great spread of a lunch and back out for an afternoon of bringing in more birds.

The experience enlightened me to be able to go on other hunts with less fancy amenities. I will never forget the hospitality of the first great experience. I arrived home Sunday night with a relaxed smile. I now see what all the hunters see — the great outdoors.

Summer Pheasant Salad

Rich and Phyllis Johnson, Central Montana PF Chapter 417, Lewistown, Montana

Ingredients:

- 1 or 2 pheasant breasts, sliced into strips
- ½ tsp. ground ginger
- ½ tsp. dried minced garlic
- 4 Tbsp. teriyaki sauce
- ¼ cup canola oil
- Black pepper to taste
- 1 bunch red leaf lettuce
- 1 bunch green leaf lettuce
- 1 cucumber, peeled and sliced
- 12 cherry tomatoes
- ½ yellow or red bell pepper, seeded and sliced very thin lengthwise
- 1 cup mozzarella cheese, grated
- Sweet honey dressing or vinaigrette of choice
- Sugar snap peas, fresh basil and cashew nuts (optional)

Step 1: Pour canola oil into a large frying pan and heat to medium-high heat. Add the pheasant and while stirring add the ginger, garlic, black pepper and the teriyaki sauce. Do not overcook the pheasant. It is done when the juices run clear when the pheasant is poked with a fork. Remove the pheasant from the fry pan and set it aside.

Step 2: Wash the vegetables and tear lettuce apart by hand. Add the rest of vegetables, 4 or 5 tablespoons of dressing and gently toss. Arrange the pheasant on top of the finished salad, sprinkle with the cheese and serve with fresh fruit of the season. Add optional ingredients as desired.

John's Aloha Pheasant and Rice

John Koegler, Great Salt Lake PF Chapter 288, Salt Lake City, Utah

Ingredients:

- 2 cups uncooked instant rice
- 2 8 oz. cans pineapple tidbits (save the juice)
- 2 cups chicken bouillon (chicken base)
- 2 green peppers, chopped
- ½ onion, chopped
- 1 pkg. Shake n' Bake original chicken seasoning coating mix
- 2 skinless and boneless pheasant breasts, cut into strips.

Step 1: Preheat oven to 400° F. Mix rice and pineapple with juice, chicken bouillon, green peppers and onion in 9×13-inch baking dish.

Step 2: Place coating mix in a plastic bag. Add pheasant strips and shake to coat evenly. Place pheasant on rice mixture and bake for 30 minutes or until the pheasant is cooked through.

Pheasant Lentil Soup

Dan and Daley Hall, Central Montana PF Chapter 417, Lewistown, Montana

Ingredients:

    4 Tbsp. butter
    3 leeks, thinly sliced
    3 carrots, chopped
    2 onions, chopped
    4 cloves garlic, finely chopped
    2 qts. chicken broth
    1 pheasant (halved)
    1 cup dried lentils
    ½ cup parsley, chopped
      Salt and pepper
    ¼ cup Madeira (wine)

Step 1: Melt butter in large soup pot over medium-low heat. Add leeks, carrots, onions and garlic. Cook 15 minutes.

Step 2: Add the stock, pheasant, lentils, half the parsley, salt and pepper. Bring to boil, reduce heat and simmer uncovered 30 minutes.

Step 3: Remove the pheasant and continue simmering the soup, uncovered 30 minutes more. Skim off any fat. When pheasant is cool, shred the meat and set aside. Discard bones.

Step 4: Add Madeira, remaining parsley and shredded meat to the soup. Adjust seasonings and heat through but do not boil. Serve hot.

Orange and Cranberry Pheasant

Garry and Leanne King, Central Montana PF Chapter 417, Lewistown, Montana

Ingredients:

    2 pheasants
      Flour
      Butter and oil for frying
    1 cup orange juice
    ¾ cup sugar
    1 cup frozen cranberries
    1 oz. Triple Sec or other orange liqueur
      Salt, pepper and poultry seasoning
        to taste
      White rice, cooked

Step 1: Debone the breast meat from two pheasants and the thigh meat from the legs. Cut the breast and thigh meat into strips, dust and cover with flour. Pan fry in a mixture of butter and oil. Cook until browned, but not overdone. Place the pheasant on a paper towel and discard the oil mixture.

Step 2: Add orange juice, sugar and cranberries to frying pan. Mix in the pheasant and simmer for 20 to 30 minutes. Add liqueur at the end of cooking. Season to taste. Serve over rice.

Fuel-Injected Pheasant

Fred Tullis, Rodeo, New Mexico
Fred is a chef at Price Canyon Dude Ranch in Douglas, Arizona.

Tip: Injecting a pheasant with a liquid marinade is a good technique to use for older birds especially. It marinates them from the inside out, making them more tender and less dry. Refrigerate the skinned whole pheasant 2 to 3 hours before injecting, allowing the butter and wine marinade to congeal more quickly upon contact with the cool meat.

Ingredients:
- 1 skinned whole pheasant, chilled
- ½ stick butter
- 5 Tbsp. white wine
- 2 tsp. garlic powder
- 3 cloves garlic, crushed
- ½ lemon, cut into 2 pieces
  Pheasant marinade (recipe to follow)
- 4 strips bacon
- 2 Tbsp. parsley, chopped
  Salt and pepper to taste

Step 1: Place chilled pheasant in a glass baking pan. Season the outside and cavity with salt and pepper. Tie legs together.

Step 2: In a small saucepan, melt butter. Add wine and garlic; simmer for 1 minute. Using a syringe and medium-gauge needle, fill pheasant with the marinade; inject it into the entire bird, fanning the needle to distribute the marinade thoroughly. Repeat until the marinade flows out of the bird. Refrigerate immediately for up to 8 hours.

Step 3: Preheat oven to 400° F. Lay bacon onto the outside of pheasant. Cover with foil and bake for 25 minutes. Remove foil and bake for another 25 minutes. Discard bacon, lemon and garlic. Quarter the pheasant and place onto serving plate. Sprinkle with parsley and garnish accordingly.

Beginner's Buck

Belinda S. Boehler, Montgomery County, Illinois, Pheasants Forever

I became a member of the Montgomery County, Illinois, Pheasants Forever beginning in 2003 upon marrying my husband. In that short time, I have become a participant in our local PF chapter as an officer and the Web master. Being a part of this group has given me wonderful insight into the outdoor world.

I first started out in 2001 learning how to shoot sporting clays with the guidance of my then future husband, along with his family and friends, who were avid shooters. From there, it evolved into trap, bird hunting and of course, deer hunting.

In November 2006, on the second day of hunting season and the first shotgun hunting weekend in Illinois, I had one of the most exciting experiences of my life, when I shot my first buck. There I was, getting ready to go to an early lunch break, and he was walking toward my stand, 100 yards away. Less than five seconds later, I shot and he ran 30 yards into the timber. What a moment that it was when I found my first buck there in the foliage, and what a prize he was. I will cherish this moment for the rest of my life.

I am so thankful not only for my husband, but to Pheasants Forever for helping me understand and take great appreciation in the outdoors and nature, while I help it to thrive and get to share in what nature provides.

Creamed Pheasant

Dan and Daley Hall, Central Montana PF Chapter 417, Lewistown, Montana

Ingredients:
- ⅓ cup all-purpose flour
- ½ tsp. salt
- ½ tsp. pepper
- ¼ tsp. lemon pepper
- ¼ tsp. garlic powder
- ¼ tsp. paprika
- 1 pheasant (cut up and skin removed)
- 3 Tbsp. oil
- 1 cup whipping cream

Step 1: Heat oven to 300° F. In large plastic food storage bag, combine flour, salt, peppers, garlic powder and paprika. Add pheasant pieces. Shake to coat.

Step 2: Heat oil in skillet over medium-high heat. Add pheasant. Cook 10 to 12 minutes or until meat is browned.

Step 3: Place pheasant pieces in 2-quart casserole. Pour cream over pheasant. Cover. Bake for 1 to 1½ hours or until meat is tender.

Pheasant and Sausage Gumbo

Jeff Walsh, Education Chairman for Southwest Washington PF Chapter 716, and wife Terry

Ingredients:
- ¼ cup margarine
- ½ cup chopped onion
- 1 clove minced garlic
- ½ yellow pepper, diced
- ½ cup celery, diced
- 2 pheasant breasts, cut up
- 1 large precooked deer sausage, cut up
- ¼ cup flour
- 4 cups chicken broth
- ¼ cup chopped parsley
- 1 pkg. frozen vegetable gumbo mix
- ½ tsp. chili powder
- ½ tsp. salt
- ¼ tsp. pepper

Step 1: Melt margarine in skillet and stir in onion, garlic, yellow pepper and celery. Sauté until almost tender. Add pheasant breasts and cook until nearly done.

Step 2: Add sausage and heat through. Stir in flour and cook for 1 minute. Slowly stir in chicken broth. Heat to boiling and cook until thickened, about 2 minutes.

Step 3: Add parsley, frozen vegetables, chili powder, salt and pepper. Cook until boiling. Serve over cooked white rice. Serves 4.

Pheasant Trivia
The nation's first pheasant season was held in 1892 in Oregon. It lasted 75 days, and 50,000 roosters were bagged.

Game Bird Rumaki

C.J. Kausel, youth education chair, Metro Denver PF Chapter

Ingredients:
Pheasant or grouse thighs, or dove
   or quail breast
Teriyaki sauce
Bacon

Step 1: Cut game bird meat into bite-size pieces. Marinate in teriyaki sauce overnight.

Step 2: Wrap each piece of meat with a half strip of bacon. Secure with toothpick.

Step 3: Bake at 375° F. for 35 to 40 minutes. Drain grease and brown for 5 minutes.

Luke's Duck

Luke Whalen, Pheasants Forever Board Member 1991-2002, Hailey, Idaho

Ingredients:
4 Tbsp. olive oil
½ cup dry white wine
6 Tbsp. teriyaki sauce
1½ Tbsp. cracked black pepper
4 Mallard duck breasts, skinless and
   boneless

Step 1: Place oil, wine and teriyaki sauce into skillet and sprinkle with 1 tablespoon of the cracked black pepper. Heat on medium-high until hot. Add breasts and cook 7 minutes.

Step 2: Turn breasts. Sprinkle the remaining pepper on top and add a dash of teriyaki sauce to each. Cook 6 more minutes. (Meat will be red on the inside.) Remove breasts and set aside.

Step 3: Reduce the sauce until slightly thickened. Slice the duck breasts thinly on the bias. Place the duck on a serving plate and spoon the sauce over the meat.

Sharp-Tailed Grouse Appetizer

Christian Cherek, Cheyenne, Wyoming

Ingredients:

    Fresh grouse breasts, as many as available or needed
1-2 Tbsp. olive oil
  1 clove of garlic, chopped
    Salt and pepper to taste
    Oregano
  1 cup red wine

Step 1: Field dress grouse as soon as possible after harvesting. Place it in a plastic bag and put in a cooler on ice. Do not freeze meat.

Step 2: After returning to the kitchen, slice grouse breast into narrow strips no more than 1 inch wide.

Step 3: Heat olive oil and garlic in skillet over medium-high heat. When oil is hot, place grouse strips in pan. Add salt, pepper and a generous supply of oregano. Stir grouse with wooden spoons for 3 to 4 minutes. The strips are perfect when blood quits running from the breasts and they are still slightly red in the middle.

Step 4: Remove strips from pan and cover with glass lid to keep hot.

Step 5: Deglaze frying pan with wine. Stir wine in pan until hot.

Step 6: Pour wine over strips of grouse breast and serve with a baguette.

Barbecued Ptarmigan

Jack Duggan, Anchorage, Alaska
Jack grew up hunting pheasants in Nebraska before moving north to Alaska.

Ingredients:

4-6 breasted ptarmigin
    Shortening
    Flour
    Salt
    Pepper
  1 large onion
  1 Tbsp. butter, melted
  1 Tbsp. brown sugar
  1 Tbsp. cornstarch
  2 Tbsp. Worcestershire sauce
  2 Tbsp. vinegar (or less)
  ½ tsp. dry mustard
  ¼ cup ketchup
  1 qt. tomatoes

Step 1: Cut ptarmigan breasts into bite-size pieces. Coat with flour, salt and pepper. Brown in shortening and place in casserole dish.

Step 2: Sauté onion in skillet with butter. Combine brown sugar and cornstarch and add to browned onion. Gradually add remaining ingredients including ¼ teaspoon salt and pepper.

Step 3: Cook sauce approximately 20 to 25 minutes. Pour sauce over browned ptarmigan and bake in casserole for 1½ hours at 300° F. Baste occasionally as necessary. Best served on pasta or bed of rice.

Elk Steaks with Mediterranean Olive Relish

Individual cuts of elk look a lot like beef except for their color. Prior to cooking, the meat is darker because it's not marbled with fat.
Prep: 30 minutes   Chill: 2 to 4 hours   Grill: 14 minutes

Ingredients:

- 3 Tbsp. olive oil
- 2 Tbsp. minced garlic (12 cloves)
- ½ tsp. salt
- ¼ tsp. black pepper
- 4 6-8-oz. elk top loin steaks
- 1 recipe Mediterranean Olive Relish (below)

Step 1: In a small bowl combine oil, garlic, salt and pepper. Brush garlic mixture over both sides of steaks. Cover and chill for 2 to 4 hours.

Step 2: For a charcoal grill, grill steaks on the rack of an uncovered grill directly over medium-hot coals until desired doneness, turning once halfway through grilling. Allow 14 to 16 minutes for medium-rare (145° F.) or 16 to 18 minutes for medium (160° F.). (For a gas grill, preheat grill. Reduce heat to medium-hot. Place steaks on grill rack over heat. Cover and grill as above.)

Step 3: Serve steaks with Mediterranean Olive Relish. Makes 4 servings.

Nutrition Facts per serving: 337 cal., 17 g total fat (3 g sat. fat), 93 mg chol., 598 mg sodium, 5 g carbo., 1 g dietary fiber, 40 g protein.
Daily Values: 0% vit. A, 40% vit. C, 3% calcium, 29% iron.

Mediterranean Olive Relish: In a small bowl combine ¼ cup chopped pitted oil-cured Greek olives or kalamata olives; 3 tablespoons chopped roasted red sweet peppers, drained; 2 tablespoons capers, drained; 1 tablespoon olive oil; 1 tablespoon lemon juice; and ⅛ teaspoon anise seeds, crushed. Cover and chill for up to 24 hours. Makes ¾ cup.

Better Homes and Gardens®

Test Kitchen

Gun Barrel BBQ Buffalo Ribs

Buffalo, also called bison, soaks up smoke flavor like nobody's business. The sauce has just the right tinge of bourbon flavor to marry well with the smoky ribs.
Prep: 20 minutes   Chill: 8 to 24 hours
Soak: 1 hour   Grill: 1¼ hours

Ingredients:
- 4 to 5 lb. buffalo ribs or beef back ribs
- 1 Tbsp. salt
- 1 Tbsp. ground black pepper
- 2 tsp. garlic powder
- 4-6 cups hickory wood chips
- ⅓ cup sorghum
- ¼ cup strong brewed coffee
- ¼ cup bourbon
- 2 Tbsp. white Worcestershire sauce
- 2 tsp. dry mustard
- 1 tsp. onion powder
- ¼ tsp. bottled hot pepper sauce
- 1½ cups ketchup

Step 1: Trim fat from ribs. For rub, in a small bowl combine salt, black pepper and garlic powder. Sprinkle rub evenly over both sides of ribs; rub in with your fingers. Cover and refrigerate for at least 8 hours or up to 24 hours.

Step 2: At least 1 hour before grilling, soak wood chips in enough water to cover. Drain before using.

Step 3: Prepare grill and wood chips for indirect grilling. Test for medium heat above the drip pan. Place ribs, bone sides down, on the grill rack over the drip pan. Cover and grill until ribs are tender. (Allow 1¼ to 1½ hours for buffalo ribs or 1 to 1¼ hours for beef ribs.) Add additional coals and wood chips as needed to maintain temperature and smoke.

Step 4: Meanwhile, for sauce, in a medium saucepan stir together sorghum, coffee, bourbon, white Worcestershire sauce, mustard, onion powder and hot pepper sauce. Bring to boiling, stirring frequently. Stir in ketchup; return sauce to boiling. Remove from heat. Remove ½ cup of the sauce; brush onto ribs twice during the last 30 minutes of grilling.

Step 5: To serve, reheat remaining sauce until bubbly; pass with ribs. Makes 4 or 5 servings.

Smoker directions: Prepare ribs as directed above. Substitute 8 to 10 hickory wood chunks for the wood chips. In a smoker arrange preheated coals, drained wood chunks and water pan according to manufacturer's directions. Pour water into pan. Place ribs, bone sides down, on grill rack over water pan. Cover and smoke until ribs are tender. (Allow 3 to 4 hours for buffalo ribs or 2½ to 3 hours for beef ribs.) Prepare sauce as directed above. Brush the ½ cup sauce on the ribs twice during the last 30 minutes of smoke cooking. Serve as directed above.

Better Homes and Gardens® Test Kitchen™

Buffalo Oven Stew

Prep: 25 minutes   Bake: 2 hours   Oven: 325° F.

Ingredients:
- 4 medium red-skinned potatoes, chopped
- 4 medium carrots, cut into 1-inch pieces, or
- 2 cups tiny whole carrots
- 1 large onion, coarsely chopped
- 1 stalk celery, sliced
- 2 Tbsp. quick-cooking tapioca
- 1 lb. buffalo (bison) or beef stew meat, cut into 1-inch cubes*
- 2 14.5-oz. cans stewed tomatoes, cut up
- 1 Tbsp. sugar
- 1 Tbsp. dried Italian seasoning, crushed (optional)
- 1 tsp. salt
- ½ tsp. black pepper

Test Kitchen

Step 1: In a 3-quart casserole, place the potatoes, carrots, onion and celery. Sprinkle tapioca over the vegetables. Add meat. In a medium bowl, combine undrained tomatoes, sugar, Italian seasoning, if you like, salt and pepper; pour over meat.

Step 2: Bake, covered, in a 325° F. oven for 2 hours or until meat is tender. Stir before serving. Makes 6 servings.

Nutrition Facts per serving: 263 cal., 3 g total fat (1 g sat. fat), 47 mg chol., 702 mg sodium, 39 g carbo., 5 g dietary fiber, 21 g protein.
Daily Values: 206% vit. A, 37% vit. C, 7% calcium, 24% iron.

Crockery-cooker directions: In a 4- to 5-quart crockery cooker, place the potatoes, carrots, onion and celery. Sprinkle tapioca over the vegetables. Add meat. In a medium bowl, combine undrained tomatoes, sugar, Italian seasoning (optional), salt and pepper; pour over meat. Cover; cook on low-heat setting for 10 to 12 hours or on high-heat setting for 5 to 6 hours.

*Recipe Note: If buffalo (bison) or beef stew meat is unavailable, use a 1½-pound buffalo (bison) or beef chuck pot roast. Trim fat from meat. Cut meat into 1-inch cubes. Continue as above.

Bacon-Wrapped Bison Ribeyes

Prep: 25 minutes Marinate: 2 to 4 hours Roast: 25 minutes Grill: 10-15 minutes Oven: 450°F.

Ingredients:

- 4 bison ribeye or beef tenderloin steaks, cut 1-inch thick (8 to 10-oz. each)
- ¼ cup soy sauce
- 2 Tbsp. olive oil
- 2 Tbsp. ketchup
- 2 tsp. snipped fresh thyme
- 1 clove garlic, minced
- ¼ tsp. dry mustard
- 4 tsp. Montreal Steak Seasoning or your favorite steak spice rub
- 8 slices hickory-smoked bacon, partially cooked
  Oven-Roasted Fingerling Potatoes (recipe follows)
  Blue cheese dip or salad dressing
- 1 large green onion, cut into thin, bias-slices
  Fresh thyme or oregano sprig (optional)
  Montreal Steak Seasoning or your favorite steak spice rub (optional)
  Steak sauce

Step 1: Trim silver skin from bison. (If using beef, trim fat from steak). Place meat in a resealable plastic bag set in a shallow dish.

Setp 2: For marinade: In a small bowl, combine soy sauce, olive oil, ketchup, snipped thyme, garlic and dry mustard. Pour over meat; seal bag. Marinate in the refrigerator for 2 to 4 hours, turning bag occasionally. Drain meat, discarding marinade. Sprinkle 4 teaspoons Montreal Spice over surface of meat; rub in with your fingers. Wrap the edge of each steak with 2 slices of partially cooked bacon, securing ends with wooden toothpicks.

Step 3: For a charcoal grill, grill steaks on the rack of an uncovered grill directly over medium coals until desired doneness, turning once halfway through grilling. Allow 10 to 12 minutes for medium-rare (145° F.) or 12 to 15 minutes for medium doneness (160° F.). (For a gas grill, preheat grill. Reduce heat to medium. Place steaks on grill rack over heat. Cover; grill as above.)

Step 4: Serve steak with the Oven-Roasted Fingerling Potatoes. Top potatoes with dip or dressing and green onions. If you like, garnish steak with a thyme or oregano sprig. Serve with additional Montreal spice, if you like, and steak sauce. Makes 4 servings.

Nutrition Facts per serving: 552 cal., 24 g total fat (7 g sat. fat), 164 mg chol., 2,136 mg sodium, 22 g carbo., 2 g dietary fiber, 59 g protein.
Daily Values: 4% vit. A, 41% vit. C, 6% calcium, 44% iron.

Oven-Roasted Fingerling Potatoes: In a greased 9×9×2-inch baking pan, place 12 fingerling potatoes, halved (small, long, and finger-shape potatoes) or 12 tiny new potatoes, halved (about 1 pound). In a small bowl, combine 2 tablespoons herb oil or olive oil and 2 teaspoons Montreal Spice (McCormick®). Drizzle over potatoes, tossing to coat. Bake in a 450° F. oven 25 to 30 minutes or until potatoes are tender and brown on the edges, stirring once.

Better Homes and Gardens®
Test Kitchen

Bison and Zucchini Burgers with Thousand Island Slaw

Prep: 45 minutes   Chill: 2 hours   Grill: 14 minutes

Ingredients:

- 1 Tbsp. olive oil
- 1 cup zucchini, finely chopped
- 1 cup onion, finely chopped (1 large)
- 1 egg, slightly beaten
- ½ cup Parmesan cheese, grated
- 2 Tbsp. snipped fresh basil or 1½ tsp. dried basil, crushed
- ½ tsp. salt
- ½ tsp. ground black pepper
- 2 lbs. ground bison, ground elk or lean ground beef
- Thousand Island Slaw (recipe follows)
- 4 large (6 to 7 inches) white or wheat pita bread rounds, halved crosswise and warmed

Better Homes and Gardens®

Test Kitchen

Step 1: In a large skillet, heat oil over medium-high heat. Add zucchini and onion and cook about 5 minutes or till vegetables are tender, stirring occasionally. Cool.

Step 2: In a large bowl, combine egg, zucchini mixture, Parmesan cheese, basil, salt and black pepper. Add bison; mix well. Shape meat mixture into eight ¾-inch-thick patties.

Step 3: For a charcoal grill: Grill patties on the rack of an uncovered grill directly over medium coals for 14 to 18 minutes or till meat is done (160° F.), turning once halfway through grilling. (For a gas grill: Preheat grill. Reduce heat to medium. Place patties on grill rack over heat. Cover and grill as above.)

Step 4: To serve, place burgers and Thousand Island Slaw inside pitas. Makes 8 servings.

Nutrition Facts per serving: 310 cal., 10 g total fat (3 g sat. fat), 108 mg chol., 545 mg sodium, 23 g carbo., 2 g dietary fiber, 32 g protein.
Daily Values: 4% vit. A, 20% vit. C, 11% calcium, 26% iron.

Thousand Island Slaw: In a medium bowl, combine 2 cups finely shredded green and/or red cabbage, 1 cup zucchini cut into thin bite-size strips, and 2 tablespoons finely chopped red onion. Pour ⅓ cup bottled Thousand Island salad dressing over cabbage mixture. Toss lightly to coat. Cover and chill for 2 to 24 hours. Stir well before serving.

Advance Tailgating Preparation: Prepare burger mixture and shape into patties as above. Prepare slaw. Store each separately in an airtight container in the refrigerator for up to 24 hours.

To Tote: Before leaving home, place containers inside a well-insulated cooler with plenty of ice or ice packs (keep at a temperature of 40° F. or below). Wrap pita bread halves in foil. At tailgating site, grill burgers as above. Add wrapped pita bred halves to grill the last few minutes of grilling to heat through, turning occasionally. Serve as above.

quick
& easy

You don't always need a fancy recipe to make a delicious dish. Here are some down-and-dirty favorites from folks who know that sometimes, simple is best.

Oven-Fried Pheasant

Jane Bryndel, Western Pennsylvania PF Chapter 630

Ingredients:
- 2 pheasants
- ½ cup mayonnaise
- ¼ cup Parmesan cheese, grated
  Seasoned bread crumbs

Step 1: Preheat oven to 350° F. Debone pheasants and cut or pound the meat until it is all about the same thickness, so it will cook fast and be finished at about the same time. Spread the meat out in the bottom of a glass baking dish.

Step 2: Mix mayonnaise and cheese and spread on the meat. Sprinkle with seasoned bread crumbs. Bake for 30 to 40 minutes or until the meat is done and bread crumbs are brown.

Pheasant and Wild Rice

Dean Turek, Habitat Chair, Rice County, Minnesota, PF Chapter 821

Ingredients:
- 2-4 pheasant breasts
  Wild rice
- 1 pkg. powdered onion soup mix
- 2 cans cream of chicken soup

Step 1: Butter bottom and sides of roasting pan and add desired amount of rice for number of people. Add pheasant breasts and sprinkle with onion soup mix.

Step 2: Add soup and liquid according to rice instructions (subtracting to allow for soup). Bake at 350° F. for 1 hour. May take longer for larger meals. If rice soaks up too much liquid during cooking, add water as needed.

Chex Pheasants

Brad Glendening, Pleasant Hill, Iowa, Dallas County PF Chapter

Ingredients:
- 2 pheasant breasts, deboned
- ½ box Corn Chex cereal
- 2 eggs
- ½ cup milk
  Butter

Step 1: Slice each pheasant breast in half, so you will have 4 thin breasts.

Step 2: Crush the cereal as finely as possible.

Step 3: Mix eggs and milk together. Dip breasts in egg mixture, then into cereal. Fry in butter until golden brown.

Pheasant Leg Dumplings
Tim Schultz, Eau Claire, Wisconsin

Never waste pheasant or wild turkey legs again! Simmer or boil until the meat falls off the bone. Set meat aside, discard bones, and run liquid through a sieve to remove unwanted material. Cut meat into bite-size pieces if needed, and place back in the liquid. Add cream of chicken or other cream soup to thicken the liquid. Make dumplings according to directions on the baking mix box. If you need more meat, chicken leg meat can be added.

Buffalo Steak in Mushroom Gravy
Carolyn Penfield, Lemmon, South Dakota

Ingredients:
4-6 buffalo round steaks, tenderized
2 cans cream of mushroom soup
1½ cans milk

Step 1: Flour and brown steaks in shortening. Place in slow cooker.

Step 2: Combine soup and milk. Add to slow cooker.

Step 3: Cook on high setting for 1 hour, then medium for 2 to 3 hours. Serve with mashed potatoes.

Pheasant Hot Dish
Dean Turek, habitat chair, Rice County, Minnesota, PF Chapter 821

Ingredients:
1-2 pheasant breasts, cooked
2 cans cream of chicken soup
1 can whipping cream
1 can peas, drained
3 cups uncooked noodles

Step 1: Cook and drain noodles.

Step 2: Combine all ingredients in slow cooker and warm until heated through. Can also be heated in the oven or on the stovetop.

Peach Marinade

Ingredients:

- ⅓ cup peach nectar
- 3 Tbsp. light teriyaki sauce
- 2 Tbsp. fresh rosemary, snipped or 2 tsp. dried rosemary, crushed
- 1 Tbsp. olive oil

In small bowl stir together peach nectar, teriyaki sauce, rosemary and olive oil. Pour over meat or fish. Turn to coat. Marinate in refrigerator at least 4 hours or up to 24 hours, turning occasionally. Drain, discarding marinade. Grill. Makes enough for ¾ pound of meat or fish.

Whiskey-Mustard Marinade

Ingredients:

- ¼ cup cooking oil
- ¼ cup whiskey
- ¼ cup stone-ground mustard
- 2 Tbsp. honey
- 2 Tbsp. vinegar
- 1 Tbsp. soy sauce
- ½ tsp. bottled hot pepper sauce
- ¼ tsp. salt

In small bowl stir together oil, whiskey, mustard, honey, vinegar, soy sauce, hot pepper sauce and salt. Pour over fish or seafood. Turn to coat. Marinate in refrigerator at least 2 hours or up to 4 hours, turning occasionally. Drain, discarding marinade. Grill. Makes enough for 2½ pounds of fish or seafood.

Sage-Orange Marinade

Ingredients:

- 1 tsp. orange peel, finely shredded
- ⅓ cup orange juice
- 2 tsp. olive oil or cooking oil
- ¾ tsp. fresh rosemary, snipped or ¼ tsp. dried rosemary, crushed
- ¾ tsp. fresh sage, snipped or ¼ tsp. dried sage, crushed
- 1 clove garlic, minced
- ¼ tsp. salt
- ¼ tsp. ground black pepper

Step 1: In a small bowl stir together orange peel, orange juice, oil, rosemary, sage, garlic, salt and pepper.

Step 2: To use, pour marinade over meat, poultry or fish in a self-sealing plastic bag set in a shallow dish; seal bag. Or pour marinade over meat, poultry or fish in a nonreactive container, such as a ceramic or glass bowl or dish. Turn to coat meat, poultry or fish. Cover if in container.

Step 3: Marinate in the refrigerator at least 6 hours or up to 12 hours. Drain meat, poultry or fish, discarding marinade. Grill. Makes about ⅓ cup marinade (enough for ¾ pound of meat).

Cilantro-Pesto Marinade

Ingredients:
- ½ cup fresh cilantro leaves, firmly packed
- ½ small red onion, chopped
- 1 tsp. lime peel, finely shredded
- 2 Tbsp. lime juice
- 2 tsp. Worcestershire sauce
- ¼ tsp. ground cumin
- ¼ tsp. dried oregano, crushed

In blender container or food processor bowl combine cilantro, onion, lime peel, lime juice, Worcestershire sauce, cumin and oregano. Cover and blend or process with a few pulses just until coarsely chopped. Pour over meat. Turn to coat. Marinate in refrigerator 1 hour, turning once. Drain meat, discarding marinade. Grill. Makes enough for 1½ pounds of meat.

Beer Marinade

Ingredients:
- 1 cup beer or apple cider*
- 2 Tbsp. brown sugar
- 1 Tbsp. Worcestershire sauce
- 2 tsp. chili powder
- 1 clove garlic, minced

Stir together the beer or cider, brown sugar, Worcestershire sauce, chili powder and garlic in a small bowl. Pour over meat in a plastic bag set in a bowl or shallow dish; close bag. Refrigerate for 4 to 24 hours. Makes about 1¼ cups (enough for 3 pounds meat).

*Note: Measure the beer after its foam has subsided.

Lemon-Garlic Marinade

Ingredients:
- ¼ cup olive oil
- 1 tsp. finely shredded lemon peel
- ¼ cup lemon juice
- 1 Tbsp. snipped fresh tarragon or 1 tsp. dried tarragon, crushed
- ½ tsp. coarsely ground black pepper
- 4 cloves garlic, minced

In a small bowl combine oil, lemon peel, lemon juice, tarragon, pepper and garlic. Pour marinade over meat in a resealable plastic bag set in a shallow dish; seal bag. Turn bag to coat. Marinate meat in the refrigerator for 1 to 2 hours. Drain, reserving marinade. Brush meat with marinade halfway through grilling. Discard remaining marinade. Makes enough for 2 pounds of meat.

Pheasant Baked in Cream
Ed Popelka, Molt, Montana, Yellowstone Valley PF Chapter

Cut pheasant into serving-size pieces and dredge in flour. Brown in enough oil to cover the bottom of the frying pan. Place browned pieces in a baking dish. Salt and pepper liberally. Pour enough whipping cream over the pheasant to cover the pieces. Bake uncovered in a 350° F. oven until cream is toast-colored and crispy.

Pheasant and Rice
Joe Anderson, Grainfield, Kansas

Cook rice, mix in some butter, and spread in the bottom of a glass cake pan. Brown pheasant breasts and place on top of the rice. Smother in cream of chicken or cream of mushroom soup, and bake at 350° F. until pheasant is completely cooked. This recipe also works well with quail.

Baked Pheasant
Ben Young, Versailles, Kentucky

Skin and cut pheasant into pieces like you would cut up a chicken. Lightly flour, salt and pepper the pieces. Brown in extra virgin olive oil in a good-size skillet. Add 1 can cream of chicken soup and a half can of water over the pieces. Brown a little more. Transfer to a covered roasting pan and bake at 325° F. for 1 hour 15 minutes or until tender. Add water if needed. Drippings in the roaster make a delicious gravy for mashed potatoes.

Lemon Pheasant
Tim Clemons, Pasco, Washington, Ringold PF Chapter

Inject lemon juice into pheasant breasts using a marinade injector, then season with salt, pepper, garlic or other seasoning. Place on a hot grill for 5 to 10 minutes until just done.

Zesty Italian Pheasant
Tim Schultz, Eau Claire, Wisconsin

Take pheasant/turkey breast meat and cut into half-inch long strips. Place in resealable plastic bag with enough oil-based zesty Italian salad dressing to coat. Marinate in the refrigerator for 1 to 24 hours, flipping bag frequently. Place on hot grill for 5 minutes per side.

Fried Quail
Cinda Brent, Marianna, Arkansas

Fry 1 to 2 quail per person in hot (450° F.) oil until golden brown. Quail may be whole or halved. We prefer frying them whole in fresh vegetable oil. This is quick and easy, and very good! Goes great with French fries or hush puppies.

Pheasant Nuggets
This is a quick and easy way to enjoy pheasant. Here, three hunters from three different states share their methods for making pheasant nuggets.

Method 1: Back to Basics
Josh Schumacher, Ames, Iowa

Mix 1 packet of Shake-n-Bake seasoning with a half to 1 cup of flour and place in resealable plastic bag. Cut pheasant meat into nuggets. Shake in plastic bag until coated, then fry in hot oil until cooked through.

Method 2: Add a Little Kick
Mark M. Sahli, founder of Dakota East Central PF, West Fargo, North Dakota

Dice 2 pheasant breasts into nugget-size pieces. Roll pieces in a packet of Shore Lunch or Shake-n-Bake. Add a dash of hot pepper sauce to each piece. Heat butter in a skillet. Add all nuggets at once, and fry until crisp. Serve with barbecue sauce, ranch dressing or your favorite dip.

Method 3: A Unique Twist
Glenn and Nancy Savage, Montgomery County, Illinois, PF Chapter 596

Ingredients:
- Pheasant
- Adolph's Meat Marinade or other tenderizing marinade
- ¾ cup white wine (may substitute water)
- Flour
- Bread crumbs
- Cornflakes cereal
- Canola oil

Step 1: Prepare the pheasant by cutting fresh or thawed breasts and or thighs into boneless nuggets. Place tenderizing marinade and white wine or water into a 1-gallon resealable plastic bag and add the pheasant pieces. Marinade from 1 to 3 hours in the refrigerator.

Step 2: In a second bag, mix equal amounts of flour, bread crumbs and crushed cornflakes. Dip the nuggets in the coating and place the nuggets into hot (325°-350° F.) canola oil. Fry until the nuggets are brown on both sides (about 3 to 5 minutes). Drain on a paper towel.

pack a snack

Hunting on an empty stomach is never a good idea — your rumbling tummy might scare the birds away. These sweet treats and savory snacks will keep you going until the dinner bell rings, and they're perfect for packing. So find a good resting spot, have a snack, then get back out there and bag those birds!

Parmesan Crisps

Ingredients:
- 4 oz. Parmesan cheese, cut into 1-inch chunks
- ¾ cup all-purpose flour
- ¼ cup cold butter, cut into 4 pieces
- 1½ tsp. lemon peel, finely shredded
- ¼ tsp. freshly ground black pepper
- 2 Tbsp. cold water
- Kosher salt or sea salt
- Lemon peel, finely shredded

Step 1: Put 2 pieces of cheese in food processor bowl fitted with chopping blade. Cover; process until cheese is almost ground. Drop in remaining cheese chunks, a few at a time, until all cheese is ground.

Step 2: Remove top; add flour, cold butter, the 1½ teaspoons lemon peel and pepper to food processor. With machine running, add water through feed tube; process until mixture just comes together. Shape into a ball.

Step 3: Preheat oven to 400° F. Flatten cheese mixture on a sheet of parchment paper. Top with parchment. Use a rolling pin to roll to a 12-inch square. Remove top sheet of parchment. Invert dough onto baking sheet; remove second parchment.

Step 4: Using fluted pastry wheel, pizza cutter, or sharp knife, cut into half-inch rectangles or half-inch-wide strips. Carefully separate dough using spatula to lift; arrange on baking sheet 1 inch apart. Using fork, prick dough. Sprinkle with salt and additional lemon peel.

Step 5: Bake for 10 to 12 minutes or until golden brown; cool on baking sheet. Makes about 48 rectangles or 24 strips.

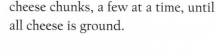

All the recipes in this section come from the Better Homes and Gardens Test Kitchen, unless otherwise noted.

Chili-Corn Snack Mix

Ingredients:
- 1 Tbsp. canola oil
- 1 Tbsp. lime juice
- 1 tsp. chili powder
- 2 cups toasted high-fiber corn cereal and/or crispy corn and rice cereal
- 1 cup tiny pretzel knots
- ½ cup whole almonds
- ¼ cup dehydrated corn kernels
- ¼ cup snipped dried apricots or whole dried cherries

Step 1: In a large skillet heat oil, lime juice, and chili powder over medium heat 30 seconds. Add cereals, pretzels and almonds. Cook 4 to 6 minutes or until cereal and almonds are very lightly browned, stirring frequently.

Step 2: Remove from heat. Stir in corn and apricots. Spread mixture on foil to cool. Makes 8 ½-cup servings.

Crisp Pasta Snacks

Ingredients:
- 6 oz. rotini (corkscrews), ditalini (tiny bow ties), ruote (wagon wheels), or other bite-size pasta
- Cooking oil for deep fat frying
- 1 cup broken walnuts, toasted
- ¼ cup pumpkin seeds, toasted
- 2 Tbsp. margarine or butter, melted
- ¼ cup grated Parmesan cheese
- 1 tsp. dried oregano, crushed
- ¼ tsp. garlic salt

Step 1: Cook pasta according to package directions; drain. Rinse with cold water; drain well and let dry.

Step 2: Heat 2½ inches of cooking oil in a deep saucepan or deep-fat fryer to 365° F. Fry pasta, about a dozen at a time, in deep, hot oil for 1½ minutes or until browned, stirring to separate pieces. Remove with slotted spoon. Drain on paper towels. Repeat with remaining pasta.

Step 3: Place drained pasta in a mixing bowl; add walnuts and pumpkin seeds. Pour margarine or butter over mixture in bowl; stir to coat. Combine Parmesan cheese, oregano and garlic salt. Sprinkle over mixture in bowl; toss. Cool. Store in an airtight container up to 3 days. Makes 6 cups (24 ¼-cup servings).

7-Grain Cereal Muffins

Ingredients:
- 1 cup 7-grain cereal
- 1 cup dried tart red cherries
- ½ cup brown sugar, packed
- ¼ cup cooking oil
- 1¼ cups buttermilk
- 1 cup whole wheat flour
- 1 tsp. baking powder
- 1 tsp. ground ginger or 1 Tbsp. crystallized ginger, finely chopped
- ½ tsp. baking soda
- ½ tsp. salt
- ½ tsp. ground nutmeg
- 1 egg, slightly beaten

Step 1: Grease 12 muffin-top cups, 6 3¼-inch (jumbo) muffin cups, or 16 2½-inch muffin cups. (Or, line standard muffin cups with paper bake cups.) Set aside. In a medium bowl combine 7-grain cereal, dried cherries, brown sugar and oil. Pour buttermilk over mixture; let stand for 30 minutes.

Meanwhile, in a large bowl combine whole wheat flour, baking powder, ginger, baking soda, salt and nutmeg. Make a well in the center of dry mixture; set aside.

Step 2: Stir beaten egg into buttermilk mixture. Add buttermilk mixture all at once to dry mixture. Stir just until moistened. Fill the muffin-top cups almost full or other muffin cups ¾ full of batter.

Step 3: Bake in a 400° F. oven about 12 minutes for muffin-top cups, about 20 minutes for 3¼-inch muffins, or 15 to 18 minutes for 2½-inch muffins or until golden. Cool on a wire rack 5 minutes. Remove from cups; serve immediately. Makes 12 muffin tops, 6 3¼-inch muffins, or 16 2½-inch muffins.

Three-B Muffins

Ingredients:

Nonstick cooking spray
1⅓ cups all-purpose flour
¾ cup buckwheat flour
¼-⅓ cup sugar
1½ tsp. baking powder
1 tsp. ground cinnamon
½ tsp. baking soda
½ tsp. salt
2 eggs, slightly beaten
1 cup butternut squash, cooked and mashed
½ cup fat-free milk
2 Tbsp. cooking oil
½ tsp. orange peel, finely shredded
¼ cup orange juice
¾ cup fresh or frozen blueberries
Rolled oats

Step 1: Spray 12 2½-inch muffin cups with nonstick spray or line with paper bake cups; set pan aside. Combine the all-purpose flour, buckwheat flour, sugar, baking powder, cinnamon, baking soda and salt in a medium mixing bowl. Make a well in the center of flour mixture; set aside.

Step 2: Combine the eggs, squash, milk, oil, orange peel and orange juice in a separate mixing bowl. Add the egg mixture all at once to the flour mixture. Stir just until moistened (batter should be lumpy). Fold in blueberries.

Step 3: Preheat oven to 400° F. Spoon batter into the prepared muffin cups, filling each almost full. Sprinkle with oats. Bake for 15 to 20 minutes or until the muffins are light brown. Cool in muffin cups on wire rack for 5 minutes. Remove from muffin cups; serve warm. Makes 12 muffins.

Sweet and Spicy Toasted Almonds

Ingredients:

8 oz. unblanched almonds or pecan halves (about 2 cups)
1½ tsp. butter (no substitutes)
1 Tbsp. finely snipped fresh thyme
1½ tsp. brown sugar
¼-½ tsp. salt
¼ tsp. ground red pepper

Step 1: Spread almonds in a single layer on a baking sheet. Bake in a 350° F. oven about 10 minutes or until nuts are lightly toasted.

Step 2: Meanwhile, melt butter in a medium saucepan over medium heat until sizzling. Remove from heat. Stir in thyme, brown sugar, salt and red pepper. Add almonds to butter mixture and toss to coat. Cool slightly before serving.

Step 3: To store, seal cooled nuts in an airtight container and store for up to 1 month in refrigerator or up to 3 months in freezer. Makes 16 ¼-cup servings.

Apple Breakfast Bars

Ingredients:
- ½ cup dried apples, snipped
- ⅓ cup honey
- ¼ cup raisins
- 1 Tbsp. brown sugar
- ⅓ cup peanut butter
- ¼ cup apple butter
- ½ tsp. ground cinnamon
- ½ cup rolled oats
- ½ cup walnuts or pecans, chopped
- ⅓ cup toasted wheat germ
- ¼ cup roasted sunflower seeds
- 2 cups cornflakes and/or wheat flakes

Step 1: In a Dutch oven combine dried apples, honey, raisins and brown sugar. Heat and stir until mixture boils; reduce heat slightly. Cook, uncovered, for 1 minute, stirring constantly. Remove from heat. Stir in peanut butter until melted. Stir in apple butter and cinnamon. Stir in rolled oats, walnuts or pecans, wheat germ and sunflower seeds until well combined. Add cereal, stirring to coat.

Step 2: Press mixture very firmly (or bars will crumble) and evenly into an ungreased 8×8×2-inch pan. Chill to set. Cut into 8 bars. Store in an airtight container in the refrigerator up to 2 days. Makes 8 bars.

Shortbread Brownies

Ingredients:
- 1 cup all-purpose flour
- ¼ cup brown sugar, packed
- ½ cup butter
- ¼ cup miniature semisweet chocolate pieces
- 1⅓ cups granulated sugar
- ¾ cup all-purpose flour
- ½ cup unsweetened cocoa powder
- 1½ tsp. baking powder
- ½ tsp. salt
- 3 eggs
- ⅓ cup butter, melted
- 1 Tbsp. vanilla
- ½ cup miniature semisweet chocolate pieces

Step 1: Preheat oven to 350° F. Line a 9×9×2-inch baking pan with foil; set aside. In a medium mixing bowl stir together 1 cup flour and the brown sugar. Cut in the ½ cup butter until mixture resembles coarse crumbs. Stir in the ¼ cup chocolate pieces. Press into prepared pan. Bake for 8 minutes.

Step 2: Meanwhile, in a large mixing bowl stir together granulated sugar, ¾ cup flour, the cocoa powder, baking powder and salt. Add eggs, melted butter and vanilla; beat by hand until smooth. Stir in the ½ cup chocolate pieces. Carefully spread over crust in pan.

Step 3: Bake 40 minutes more. Cool brownies in pan on a wire rack. Lift brownies out of pan by lifting up on foil. Cut into bars. Makes 24 bars.

One-Handed Fried Pies

Ingredients:
- ¾ cup dried peaches, apricots, and/or apples (3 oz.)
- ⅔ cup apple cider
- 1 cup all-purpose flour
- 1 tsp. granulated sugar
- 1 tsp. baking powder
- ⅛ tsp. baking soda
- ⅛ tsp. salt
- ¼ cup shortening
- ⅓-½ cup buttermilk
- Water
- 2 Tbsp. shortening
- Sifted powdered sugar

Step 1: For filling, in a small saucepan, combine dried fruit and apple cider. Bring to boiling; reduce heat. Cover and simmer for 20 to 25 minutes or until fruit is tender and cider is nearly absorbed. Mash slightly; cool.

Step 2: Meanwhile, for pastry, in a medium bowl stir together flour, granulated sugar, baking powder, baking soda and salt. Using a pastry blender, cut in the ¼ cup shortening until pieces are pea-size. Sprinkle buttermilk, 1 tablespoon at a time, over flour mixture, gently tossing with a fork between additions and pushing mixture to side of bowl. (Add only enough buttermilk to moisten all of the mixture.) Form dough into a ball.

Step 3: On a lightly floured surface, roll dough into a 15-inch circle. Using a 4-inch round cutter, cut the dough into 6 circles, rerolling dough as needed. Place about 1 tablespoon of the filling on half of each circle. Moisten edges of pastry circles with a little water. Fold circles over filling, creating half-moon shapes; seal edges with a fork.

Step 4: In a 12-inch nonstick skillet, heat the 2 tablespoons shortening over medium-low heat. Fry the pies for 8 to 10 minutes or until golden brown, turning once. Drain on paper towels. Serve warm. Sprinkle with powdered sugar before serving. Makes 6 servings.

Make-Ahead Tip: Prepare and fry pies as directed; cool. Place pies in layers separated by waxed paper in an airtight container and freeze for up to 3 weeks. Preheat oven to 350° F. Wrap the frozen pies individually in foil and bake about 25 minutes or until heated through. Sprinkle with powdered sugar before serving.

Irish Coffee Brownies

Ingredients:
- 1¼ cups granulated sugar
- ¾ cup butter or margarine, softened
- ½ cup unsweetened cocoa powder
- 2 eggs
- 1 tsp. vanilla
- 1½ cups all-purpose flour
- 1 tsp. baking powder
- ¼ tsp. baking soda
- ¾ cup milk
- ¼ cup Irish whiskey
- 2 Tbsp. instant coffee crystals
- 1 cup chopped walnuts
- 2½ cups sifted powdered sugar
- 2 Tbsp. unsweetened cocoa powder
- 1 Tbsp. Irish Whiskey
- 1¼ tsp. vanilla
- 3-4 Tbsp. brewed coffee
  Chopped walnuts (optional)

Step 1: Heat granulated sugar, butter or margarine and ½ cup cocoa powder in a large saucepan over medium heat until butter or margarine melts, stirring constantly. Remove from heat. Add eggs and 1 teaspoon vanilla; beat lightly just until combined.

Step 2: Stir together flour, baking powder and baking soda in a bowl; set aside. Stir together milk and ¼ cup whiskey; stir in coffee crystals. Add flour mixture and milk mixture alternately to the chocolate mixture, beating by hand after each addition. Stir in nuts. Pour into a greased 15×10×1-inch baking pan.

Step 3: Bake in a 350° F. oven for 15 to 20 minutes or until a toothpick inserted near the center comes out clean. Cool in pan on a wire rack.

Step 4: Meanwhile, for the Irish Coffee Glaze, stir together sifted powdered sugar, 2 tablespoons unsweetened cocoa powder, 1 tablespoon Irish whiskey and 1¼ teaspoons vanilla. Stir in 3 to 4 tablespoons brewed coffee until of drizzling consistency.

Step 5: If desired, sprinkle with additional chopped nuts. Makes 36 brownies.

Peanut Butter Sandwich Cookies

Ingredients:
- ½ cup creamy peanut butter
- ¼ cup butter or margarine
- ¼ cup shortening
- 1 cup brown sugar, packed
- 1 tsp. baking powder
- 1 egg
- 1 tsp. vanilla
- 1¼ cups all-purpose flour
- ¼ cup butter or margarine, softened
- ⅓ cup creamy peanut butter
- 3 cups sifted powdered sugar
- ½ tsp. vanilla
- Milk

Step 1: Beat in ½ cup peanut butter, ¼ cup butter or margarine and shortening in a large mixing bowl with an electric mixer on medium speed for 30 seconds. Add brown sugar and baking powder; beat until combined. Beat in egg and 1 teaspoon vanilla. Beat in as much of the flour as you can with the mixer. Stir in remaining flour with a wooden spoon. Divide dough in half. Wrap and chill for 2 hours or until easy to handle. (Dough can be chilled overnight.)

Step 2: Roll out each portion of dough on a lightly floured surface until ⅛ inch thick. Transfer a peanut-shape pattern to heavy paper. Place pattern on dough and cut out with a sharp knife. Place cutouts 1 inch apart on an ungreased cookie sheet.

Step 3: Bake on a cooke sheet in a 350° F. oven for 8 to 10 minutes or until bottoms are lightly browned. Transfer cookies to wire racks to cool.

Step 4: For the frosting, in a medium bowl beat together ¼ cup butter and ⅓ cup creamy peanut butter until combined. Beat in powdered sugar, ½ teaspoon vanilla and enough milk (3 to 4 teaspoons) to make spreading consistency. Drizzle over sandwiches. Makes about 36 sandwich cookies.

Tip: For the peanut-shape pattern, the peanut shape should be 4 inches long, 1½ inches wide, and with an indention of 1¼ inches in width in the center.

Ranger Cookies

Ingredients:
- 1¼ cups all-purpose flour
- ½ tsp. baking powder
- ¼ tsp. baking soda
- ½ cup shortening that doesn't require refrigeration
- 2 cups fruit-flavor crisp rice cereal
- ⅔ cup brown sugar, packed
- ⅓ cup coconut
- 1 egg, beaten
- 2 Tbsp. milk
- 1 tsp. vanilla

Step 1: Stir together the flour, baking powder and baking soda in a medium mixing bowl. Cut in shortening until the mixture resembles coarse crumbs.

Step 2: Layer in a 1-quart glass jar or canister the following ingredients: half of the cereal, flour mixture, brown sugar, remaining cereal and coconut. Tap jar gently on the counter to settle each layer before adding the next. Cover jar.

Step 3: Store at room temperature up to 1 month. Or, attach baking directions and give as a gift.

Step 4: Baking directions: Heat oven to 375° F. Empty contents of jar into a large mixing bowl. Stir in egg, milk and vanilla until combined. Drop by rounded teaspoons 2 inches apart onto an ungreased cookie sheet. Bake for 8 to 9 minutes or until edges are golden brown. Cool on cookie sheet for 1 minute. Transfer to wire racks and cool. Makes 24 cookies.

Banana-Raisin Trail Mix

Ingredients:
- 2 cups raisins
- 2 cups dried banana chips
- 2 cups unsalted dry roasted peanuts
- 1 6-oz. pkg. mixed dried fruit bits (1⅓ cups)

Step 1: In a storage container combine raisins, banana chips, peanuts and fruit. Store in a cool, dry place for up to 1 week. (To tote, take the container or divide among small resealable plastic bags.) Makes about 7 cups (14 ½ cup servings).

Make-Ahead Tip: Prepare the mix. Store, covered, in a cool, dry place up to 1 week.

Grandma Helen's Oh Henry Bars

Lisa Foust Prater, Book Editor, Rosemount, Iowa

Ingredients:
- 1 cup sugar
- 1 cup white syrup
- 1 cup peanut butter
- 7 cups Special K or similar cereal
- 2 cups chocolate chips

Step 1: Stir sugar, syrup and peanut butter over low heat and bring to a boil.

Step 2: Place cereal in a large bowl. Pour melted mixture over cereal, stir to coat, and spread in pan.

Step 3: Melt chocolate chips, and spread over mixture in pan. Cool and cut into squares.

Peanut Butter Breakfast Bars

Ingredients:
    Nonstick cooking spray
  4 cups sweetened oat cereal flakes with raisins
  ¾ cup quick-cooking rolled oats
  ½ cup all-purpose flour
  ½ cup snipped dried apples
  2 eggs, slightly beaten
  ⅓ cup honey
  ⅓ cup chunky peanut butter
  ¼ cup butter, melted, or cooking oil

Step 1: Preheat oven to 325° F. Line a 9×9×2-inch baking pan with foil. Coat foil with nonstick spray; set aside. In a large bowl combine cereal, rolled oats, flour and dried apples. Set aside.

Step 2: In a small bowl stir together eggs, honey, peanut butter and melted butter. Pour over cereal mixture. Mix well. Transfer mixture to prepared pan. Using the back of a large spoon, press mixture firmly into pan. Bake in preheated oven for 28 to 30 minutes or until edges are browned. Cool completely on a wire rack. Cut into bars using a serrated knife. Makes 16 servings.

Chewy Granola Goodies

Ingredients:
  1 10-oz. bag regular marshmallows
  ¼ cup butter or margarine
  4 cups granola with raisins
  1½ cups crisp rice cereal
  ½ cup sunflower nuts

Step 1: Line a 9×13-inch pan with foil. Butter foil. Set aside.

Step 2: In a large saucepan combine the marshmallows and butter. Cook and stir mixture until the marshmallows are melted.

Step 3: Stir in granola with raisins, crisp rice cereal, and sunflower nuts.

Step 4: Press mixture into the prepared pan. Cool. Remove foil lining with uncut bars from pan. Cut into bars. Makes 24 servings.

Two-Way Maple-Peanut Mix

Ingredients:
- 1 cup maple syrup
- 2 Tbsp. butter, melted
- 8 cups cocktail peanuts
- 1-1½ tsp. ground red pepper
- 3 cups pretzel sticks
- 1 cup dried cranberries
- 1 6-oz. bar milk chocolate, broken into bite-size pieces

Step 1: Line two 15×10×1-inch baking pans with foil. Grease foil, set aside. In a bowl stir together syrup and butter; stir in peanuts. Place half of the mixture (4 cups) in a single layer in one baking pan. Stir ground red pepper into remaining mixture in bowl; place in a single layer on second baking pan. Bake, uncovered, in a 350°F. oven for 20 minutes, stirring twice. Stir 1½ cups pretzels and the cranberries into the half with the crushed red pepper. Stir remaining pretzels into the other mixture. Coat two large sheets of heavy foil with nonstick cooking spray. Spoon mixture onto the foil. Cool competely. Break into clusters.

Step 2: Transfer the cranberry mixture into one serving bowl. Add chocolate to remaining mixture; transfer to a second serving bowl. Serve, or store, tightly covered, up to 5 days. Makes 32 ½ cup servings.

Caramel Corn Party Mix

Prep: 15 minutes Bake: 20 minutes

Ingredients:
- 4 cups popped popcorn
- 2 cups bite-size wheat or bran square cereal
- 1½ cups small pretzels or pretzel sticks
- 1½ cups pecan halves
- ¾ cup brown sugar, packed
- 6 Tbsp. butter (no substitutes)
- 3 Tbsp. light-color corn syrup
- 1 tsp. pumpkin pie spice
- ¼ tsp. baking soda
- ¼ tsp. vanilla
- Dash ground red pepper

Step 1: Heat oven to 300°F. Remove all unpopped kernels from popped popcorn. Combine popcorn, cereal, pretzels and pecans in a 17×12×2-inch baking or roasting pan.

Step 2: Mix brown sugar, butter and corn syrup in a medium saucepan. Cook and stir with a wooden spoon over medium heat until mixture boils. Reduce heat to medium-low. Cook without stirring for 5 minutes more.

Step 3: Remove pan from heat. Stir in pumpkin pie spice, baking soda, vanilla and red pepper. Pour over popcorn mixture in pan, gently stirring to coat. Bake for 15 minutes. Stir mixture; bake 5 minutes more. Spread caramel corn mixture on a large piece of buttered foil to cool. Break into pieces. Store tightly covered up to 1 week. Makes about 8 cups.

for the dogs

No hunting party is complete without a faithful canine companion or two. Their unbridled excitement at heading out for a hunt is contagious — they really know how to work and have fun at the same time. But dogs are more than just assistants in the field. They're part of the family.

Peanut Butter Acorns For Dogs

Lisa Foust Prater, Book Editor, Rosemount, Iowa

Ingredients:
- 1 cup oatmeal, uncooked
- ½ cup peanut butter
- 1½ cups hot water
- ¾ cup powdered milk
- ¾ cup cornmeal
- 1 egg, beaten
- 3 cups whole wheat flour

Step 1: Place oats and peanut butter in large bowl. Pour hot water over top. Let stand 5 minutes.

Step 2: Add powdered milk, egg and cornmeal. Stir. Add flour, ½ cup at a time, stirring after each addition. Mixture will be very thick and may require a little extra water.

Step 3: Roll mixture into sheets, cut with acorn-shaped cookie cutter, and place on baking sheet sprayed with nonstick cooking spray.

Step 4: Bake at 300° F. for 50 minutes.

It's All About Dog Work
Carl Altenbernd, Sabin, Minnesota

For me, hunting is all about the dog work. I hunt most of the time by myself with a minimum of three dogs, but going with five or six is a thrill. Two years ago I got drawn for the Minnesota prairie chicken hunt. It was a slightly windy day, so mid-day I took Teal, Breeze and Ruff, and we worked a big pasture area. The dogs got hot in the middle of the complex, and up flushes a rooster.

We doubled back in the field and they flushed a second rooster. I just winged it and it sailed out into a big open area.

As I watched the dogs do their mark and retrieve, a prairie chicken jumped up off the ground about three feet and settled back down about 150 yards in front of the dogs. As the dogs were running after the crippled bird, I was thinking I had just screwed up my chicken hunt by shooting a few pheasants.

The dogs quickly brought the bird back and we hustled out to the jump spot, and up jumped 50 to 60 prairie chickens from 50 to 150 yards in front of us. The hunt was over. What a great hunt and memory!

Skunk-Off Dog Destinker

Bill Zehnder, Frankenmuth, Michigan

Ingredients:
- 1 Tbsp. liquid dish detergent
- ½ cup baking soda
- 1 qt. peroxide

Step 1: Mix together and lather on wet dog. After 15 minutes, rinse off.

Step 2: Try to keep dog away from additional skunks.

Worth the Wait
Kirk Augustine, Omaha, Nebraska

My hunting experiences started in the heyday of Southern Iowa pheasant country in the mid-1960s. In those days, bird dogs were really not too necessary. A boy with a single-shot 20-gauge could walk small ditches, grassways, and fence rows and have a chance to limit-out in three hours.

Still, it always seemed to me the hunts that included dogs were much more fun and exciting, and I dreamed of the time when I would have my own dogs.

Years later, as my daughter approached her 12th birthday, my wife wanted to get her a golden retriever. Of course, I was quick to agree thinking that finally my hunting dog might be within reach. And my son, then 15, thought this hunting thing would be pretty neat too, now that we had a dog!

I started working with the golden on some basics and she seemed to get it. As it turned out, she was a great walking companion, but had little if any sense of smell … so much for the dream.

A few years later, we added a beautiful Vizsla to the family. This dog had loads of natural talent. I finally had my dream dog! On the inaugural hunt, the first point was beautiful. A big rooster flushed and all of the guys in the party shot. Turns out the dog was gun shy.

As time passed, our grown children moved out of the house, and the old golden and I simply looked at one another and enjoyed each other's company.

When our son got married, his wife wanted a big dog. I found a litter of lab-shorthair cross pups that were an accident, and the price was right. The dream was alive again and I now had a grandpuppy, Costa.

When he was about 4½ months old, we took him on his first hunt, for chukars. He hunted, pointed, and found downed birds. The problem was he wouldn't give them up until he had thoroughly devoured them.

Four months later, we tried again. After a few more retrieves, the dog would pick up the bird and without a whistle or command, bring it straight to my son's feet and drop it. What a sight!

The retrieve of the day came when a chukar blasted out of his cover 20 yards ahead of the dog, and I broke a wing at 70 yards on the last of our four shells. The bird coasted over the hill with Costa hot on his tail. Neither of us could see the pup but we decided to trust him. After a minute or two, my son blasted the whistle to come, and over the hill came Costa, carrying a very alive bird. No way! A 150-yard downed bird, blind landing, followed by a live retrieve. What a sight!

Bacon Cheeseburger Pizza Bones

Lisa Foust Prater, Book Editor, Rosemount, Iowa

Ingredients:
- 1 cup uncooked oatmeal
- ¼ cup bacon bits
- ½ cup hot water
- 1 3-oz. can tomato sauce
- ½ cup powdered milk
- 1 cup cheddar cheese, grated
- 1 egg, beaten
- ¾ cup cornmeal
- 2 cups whole wheat flour

Step 1: Heat water and tomato sauce until bubbly. Place oats in large bowl. Pour heated mixture over oats. Let stand 5 minutes.

Step 2: Add egg, powdered milk, cheese and bacon; stir. Add cornmeal; stir.

Step 3: Add flour, ½ cup at a time, mixing well after each addition. As the dough becomes thicker, knead remaining flour into mixture.

Step 4: Roll mixture into sheets, cut with bone-shaped cookie cutter, and place on baking sheet sprayed with nonstick cooking spray. Bake at 350°F. for 35 minutes.

The Cross-Eyed Miracle

Richard Olson, Bismarck, North Dakota

I was almost ashamed of the grief I felt. Rip, my hunting dog companion of over 13 years, had just been buried. A German shorthair pointer, he had been failing for many months before my good wife helped me make the proper decision to have him put down. We buried him at the family ranch cabin, in the wide open spaces he'd loved so much.

I called a German shorthair breeder, but he had sold his last pup. Then he asked if I'd consider a grown dog. In a flash, I imagined going hunting that fall with a fully trained dog and no puppy problems.

The breeder had three dogs available. Two were fully trained and ready to go, with a price tag of $600 each. The third dog was untrained and slightly cross-eyed. "If you're willing to take a chance, I'll sell him for $175," the breeder said. I was almost surprised to hear myself saying I'd buy the dog, and I picked him up two weeks later.

I snapped a leash on Rip II and he surprised me by docilely walking to my car with me. He hopped in the back and immediately lay down behind the driver's seat. When I climbed in, he placed his head gently on my right shoulder and closed his eyes. I was a goner.

On Rip's first trip to the field, I let him out of the pickup truck, locked the door, and turned to see him frozen on point. He had happened on a large covey of grouse. His eyes blazed with intensity, one front paw raised, and his body quivered from the glory of all that bird scent. I walked about 25 yards ahead of him and flushed the grouse. It was a great beginning for a new dog. He made 26 separate points that day without flushing one bird, and I'd never uttered one word nor blown a whistle. I had myself a natural.

One of his most-told hunting stories happened along the Missouri River south of Bismarck. A wily old rooster flushed wild several yards ahead of us and flew to safety in a cattail slough about 500 yards away. We worked the dog into the area, but since the cattails were shoulder-high and very dense, Rip had to leap in great bounds in order to make progress. As we got closer, he leaped in a high bound that would have carried him beyond the pheasant. In mid-air, he caught the bird's scent and froze in a pointing posture with his head in the bird's direction over his shoulder. The crash when he fell into the cattails flushed the bird, and we filled our limit for the day.

One day after Rip had lived with us for a year or more, my wife, Nancy, said, "Look, his eyes aren't crossed any longer!" Apparently time had corrected the problem. Nancy disagrees though. She says love did it. Now that's a miracle.

Cheesy Cow Treats for Hunting Dogs

Lisa Foust Prater, Book Editor, Rosemount, Iowa

Ingredients:
- ¾ cup beef broth
- ⅓ cup margarine
- ½ cup powdered milk
- 1 egg, beaten
- 1 cup shredded cheese, whichever variety your dog prefers
- ½ cup cornmeal
- ½ cup wheat germ
- 2¼ cups whole wheat flour
- 2 Tbsp. garlic powder

Step 1: Place margarine in large bowl. Pour hot beef broth over margarine; let stand 5 minutes.

Step 2: Stir in powdered milk, egg, garlic powder and cheese. Add corn meal and wheat germ; mix well.

Step 3: Add flour, ½ cup at a time, mixing well after each addition. This will form a very stiff dough. Knead 3 to 4 minutes.

Step 4: Roll out dough and cut with cow-shape cookie cutter. Place on a greased baking sheet. Brush with beef broth. Bake at 350° F. for 35 minutes.

Step 5: Give your dog a treat!

Innocent Eyes

Jason Hart, Iowa

I recently had a long-time hunting partner pass in a car accident. Here's a photo of my buddy, Alec "Cully" Christianson (left), and the rest of our group at the Butler County, Iowa, opening day hunt in 1994. Thinking about Alec brought back memories of a poem my mother, Gwen Hart, penned about my older brother and his dog. I thought it would make a nice tribute to Cully, and all of the other great hunting partners who have left us, whether they had two or four legs. Here's an excerpt:

A boy and his dog with innocent eyes
together they grew, each forming their ties

Together they grew and good friends they were
and hunting was fun with a dog such as her

Old Hope had her place, the front seat was great
"I'm people," she thought, "and I'm out for a date."

The sight was familiar as they drove down the road
both looked to the ditch, the gun ready to load

Together they found many pheasants to kill
the "hunt" more important than their limit to fill

As long days were done, so many's the time
they curled up as one by the warm burning pine

Twelve summers have gone, their friendship complete
a boy and his dog, their love hard to beat

A boy and his dog with innocent eyes
the dog went to heav'n, the young boy just sighs.

index

index